MOMENTS OF HAPPINESS

MOMENTS OF HAPPINESS

A Wisconsin Band Story

Mike Leckrone and Doug Moe

THE UNIVERSITY OF WISCONSIN PRESS

Publication of this book has been made possible, in part, through support
from the Anonymous Fund of the College of Letters and Science
at the University of Wisconsin–Madison
and an anonymous foundation.

The University of Wisconsin Press
728 State Street, Suite 443
Madison, Wisconsin 53706
uwpress.wisc.edu

Printed in the United States of America
This book may be available in a digital edition.

Library of Congress Cataloging-in-Publication Data

Names: Leckrone, Michael, author. | Moe, Doug, author.
Title: Moments of happiness : a Wisconsin Band story / Mike Leckrone and Doug Moe.
Description: Madison, Wisconsin : The University of Wisconsin Press, 2024.
Identifiers: LCCN 2024002388 | ISBN 9780299348809 (cloth)
Subjects: LCSH: Leckrone, Michael. | University of Wisconsin—Madison.
Varsity Band. | Band directors—Wisconsin—Madison—Biography. | Marching bands—
Wisconsin—Madison. | LCGFT: Autobiographies.
Classification: LCC ML422.L363 A3 2024 | DDC 784.8/30977583—dc23/eng/20240121
LC record available at https://lccn.loc.gov/2024002388

Dedicated to the Wisconsin band—
"Eat a rock!"

To my family, who gave me time to do
what I wanted to do.

And to Phyllis, my life's love—
"Keep the music playing."

Life isn't about being happy all the time.

It just doesn't work that way.

In life there's pain, struggle, and sadness.

But through the struggles, the sweat, and the tears, you have the moments. That's what makes this life worth living—the moments of happiness.

—M. L.

Contents

Foreword

PAT RICHTER

I was a fan of Mike Leckrone and his University of Wisconsin Marching Band before we worked together, and I really got to know him.

We'd missed each other in Madison in the 1960s. After playing with the Badgers, I was drafted by Washington in the NFL and played eight seasons there before eventually returning to Madison and joining Oscar Mayer Foods Corporation in 1972.

Mike landed in Madison in 1969. As the next decade went on, it was impossible not to notice he was doing something special with the marching band. Although the Badgers fielded some reasonably good football teams in the 1970s, people often mentioned the band's halftime performances—and soon the postgame Fifth Quarter—as an equally compelling component of Camp Randall Saturdays.

By the second half of the 1980s, UW's football fortunes had bottomed out. We used to joke that at least people stayed until halftime to watch the band. If the Badgers' offense didn't get a first down to start the third quarter, people went home and raked leaves. There were a lot of well-groomed lawns in Madison in those days.

When I returned to UW as athletic director in 1989, I got to know Mike and appreciate how he expected hard work and excellence from his band members, while encouraging them to have fun too.

By the time we went to the 1994 Rose Bowl, the band had gained a national reputation. I recall it made one Rose Bowl official a bit nervous. I don't know what stories he'd heard but he asked me, "Are they going to fire a cannon?"

I said, "Just watch their performance. They'll knock you out."

And they did. They wowed all of Southern California.

Across Mike's time—fifty years!—they added new wrinkles. We'd occasionally tease him and ask if it was going to be *Jesus Christ Superstar* or *Phantom of the Opera* this week. The varsity band concerts at the Field House and the Kohl Center began selling out, with everyone anticipating what kind of crazy entrance Mike would make that year.

Mike was in demand across the Midwest as a speaker at UW Founders' Day events and other gatherings. He emceed our Chicago Badger Booster Club golf outing at least once while I was athletic director. It's an important fundraiser, and Mike's jokes—so bad they were good— put everyone in high spirits.

Mike speaks often about "moments of happiness" and how important it is to bank those good memories to draw on when life gets tough.

What sometimes gets lost is how many of those moments Mike and his band members provided for others with their performances. How many Rose Bowl experiences were richer for having seen the band on the pier in Santa Monica or at a Century Plaza pep rally?

The answer is: countless. The great thing—it's clear in the pages that follow—is that those were magical moments for Mike and the band too.

A lifetime's worth.

Pat Richter was a standout three-sport athlete at the University of Wisconsin and served as director of athletics from 1989 to 2004.

MOMENTS OF HAPPINESS

one

ROSES

When the routine becomes electrifying, you know it's a moment to remember.

On the afternoon I'm recalling now—January 1, 1994—I was standing outside a football stadium in my job as director of the University of Wisconsin Marching Band.

It was the start of my twenty-fifth year with the UW band. I came to Madison from Butler University in Indiana with my wife, Phyllis, and our children, in 1969.

Over the years I'd watched our Badger band members line up, four across, at stadiums in football hotbeds like Columbus and Ann Arbor. We did it at home games, too, marching from Union South into Camp Randall Stadium to take our positions in the tunnel. Entering the stadium was no big deal. The fun came later.

But then, we'd never before positioned ourselves under the famous Rose Bowl sign in Pasadena, California. The football Badgers were about to play UCLA in the most storied postseason bowl game of them all.

Already, the week—Wisconsin's first trip to the Rose Bowl in three decades—had been memorable. The band—279 strong—flew to California on a charter on Monday, December 27. We stayed at the Double-Tree hotel in Santa Monica because it was located adjacent to Santa Monica High School, which meant we could walk out the door to a practice field, which we did, every morning. We'd rehearse from 8 a.m. to 9:30 or 10 a.m. and then get on a bus to go to a performance.

Tuesday, we played at Knott's Berry Farm; Wednesday was Disneyland (a performance taped for CBS Television); on Thursday we soared in front of a huge pep rally—twenty thousand crazed Badger fans!—at the Century Plaza Hotel in Century City; and Friday we were at Universal Studios.

Later I thought that, ordinarily, if we'd had just one of those experiences, we'd have said, "What a great trip." During Rose Bowl week, the hits kept coming.

The topper was marching in the Tournament of Roses Parade early on the morning of January 1. It was high visibility and high pressure. I'd sought the advice of other band directors, who told me to work on conditioning—the parade route is five-and-a-half miles long—and to pay special attention to the difficult turn from Orange Grove Boulevard onto Colorado Boulevard, where it would be easy to get disoriented. Back in Madison we spent probably forty-five minutes of every rehearsal just working on the parade.

We learned that the cameras are focused on the first thirty minutes of the parade. The organizers encouraged us to do our strongest material up front. We were told we'd see a sign that read "TV cameras end." They didn't suggest music for us but asked for a song list, not wanting any copyright issues. Most of our stuff—"On, Wisconsin!," "If You Want to Be a Badger"—was in the public domain, though we wound up paying a royalty for playing "You've Said It All."

One parade official told me that once we passed the TV cameras, we could play whatever we wanted, or not play at all.

"Maybe just play when you see patches of your fans in the stands," he said.

He didn't realize that our fans were *everywhere* that week, including lining the entire parade route. Wisconsin had been waiting thirty years for the Badgers to go to the Rose Bowl, and when it happened, tens of thousands of state residents and UW alumni around the globe wanted in. They launched a full-out invasion of Southern California.

Standing outside the Rose Bowl Stadium that afternoon, I mentioned to the band members that they should be sure to store what was about to happen in their memory banks. But we really had no idea. It seemed as if everyone in the Rose Bowl was wearing red. When we came through the tunnel and the crowd had its first glimpse of the band, the sound was almost like an explosion.

It was an exhilarating moment I'll never forget.

Even before the Rose Bowl, the 1993 fall season had been filled with remarkable events. Barry Alvarez was in his fourth year as head football coach at Wisconsin—still early in what would be a legendary career—and the Badgers opened with six straight wins.

A disappointing loss at Minnesota followed, but then on October 30, back home at Camp Randall, the Badgers beat mighty Michigan, 13–10, for the first time since 1981.

It should have been a joyous occasion, but as the game concluded and the end zone student section fans rushed down toward the field to celebrate, the first wave was pinned against the field's guardrails by those pushing from behind. It was an ugly scene. There were numerous injuries, some serious.

The band was never in real jeopardy. We'd just started to assemble under the north goalpost for our Fifth Quarter performance when Gary Moore, a UW–Madison police officer who served as liaison to the band, came up and told me to get the band out of there. Young fans were climbing on the goalpost; the crush had begun. We made it into the tunnel and then marched out of the stadium to the Humanities Building on campus, where we dismissed on football Saturdays. Keeping the band members together was always an important part of our band protocol. We didn't want any stragglers, though I heard later that a couple of band members helped pull some students out of the collapsed fencing.

What I felt at first—before I knew the extent of the injuries at the stadium—was disappointment that we'd not been able to play our postgame show after such a tremendous win. It was the first time that had happened since the Fifth Quarter originated in 1978, after another stirring Badgers' victory.

On that late September Saturday, Wisconsin had fallen behind Oregon, 19–7, with just seven minutes left in the game. Many in the crowd of sixty-four thousand fans at Camp Randall began to file out.

But the Badgers, led by quarterback Mike Kalasmiki, stormed back, scoring twice in those final minutes, securing a 22–19 Wisconsin win.

All three of the Badgers' fourth-quarter touchdowns were preceded by the band playing "You've Said It All," a polka-like song better known to those outside of Wisconsin as a popular theme song for Budweiser beer. When that Oregon game ended, Kalasmiki and many of his teammates stayed on the field. About two hundred students joined them—safely. The band jumped into the act, too, playing a postgame "You've Said It All" and more. The Fifth Quarter was born.

We'd been playing "You've Said It All" for seven years by then. It started at a Badger hockey game at the Dane County Coliseum. The year was 1972. College hockey had begun to catch on in Madison under a charismatic coach named Bob Johnson. The coliseum's plush red seats—and, not incidentally, the beer garden downstairs—were filled with fans cheering for the Badgers.

The band had also begun to catch on. I'd been in Madison three years by then and felt having a varsity band—sometimes called a pep band, a name I never liked—presence at the Badger basketball and hockey games was important. It made friends for the band. The spirit was catching.

"You can tell it," *Wisconsin State Journal* sports editor Glenn Miller wrote in January 1971. "The fans—just like this sports editor—have noticed it. We have gone from last to first in the Big 10 in the field of pep bands."

The students came early to those hockey games, and the coliseum was usually rocking by the time our varsity band arrived. It was when we were playing at one of the breaks between periods that a group of fans—I can still remember the section they were in, GG in the upper deck—started chanting, "We want a polka! We want a polka!"

I was still fairly new to Wisconsin, or I would have already had us playing a polka. We had the Budweiser song in our repertoire, but the arrangement wasn't really a polka. I had them change the drum part a bit, so it sounded like a polka. The fans in GG clapped along and a few of them danced. Of course, at one point in the next game, they started yelling again.

"We want a polka!"

That time—or maybe it was a game or two later—the fans in GG, when we arrived at the end, sang, "When you say Bud-wei-ser, you've said it all."

When I heard that, I huddled with the band and told them the next time we played it, I wanted them to stand, turn and face section GG, and sing, "When you say WIS-CON-SIN, you've said it all."

For a game or two, it was a back-and-forth between section GG and the band. But before long we won them over. The rest of the crowd joined in: "When you say WIS-CON-SIN, you've said it all."

Half a century later, it's still one of the band's signature songs.

Funny, but when we played at Disneyland during Rose Bowl week, they asked us not to play "You've Said It All." I was never certain whether it was the commercial association or because it was specifically associated with a beer, but we agreed not to play it at Disneyland.

That California trip wasn't the only major journey the band made in late 1993, and it certainly wasn't the longest.

In early December, seventy members of the UW Marching Band and I accompanied Barry Alvarez and the Badgers to Tokyo, Japan, where the team would face Michigan State in an unusual finale to the regular season. If the Badgers beat the Spartans, Wisconsin would go to the Rose Bowl.

The game—officially titled the Coca-Cola Bowl—had been hatched a couple of years earlier when Alvarez, saying he felt he owed his players a "special" game, agreed—with the blessing of Athletic Director Pat Richter and Chancellor Donna Shalala—to give up a home game in the 1993 season. A guaranteed payday of $400,000 was a significant factor in everyone's decision to play in Tokyo.

I'd been involved since before the start of the '93 school year, when I was called to a meeting in New York City with the Japanese organizers

of the game. It turned out they wanted our band to play at halftime of
the game with a popular Japanese boy band called Ninja. The organizers gave me music they wanted us to practice and sent arrangements
they wanted us to record.

We flew to Tokyo in a jumbo jet big enough that both the Wisconsin
and Michigan State teams and bands were on it. Alvarez had been to
Tokyo previously for a college all-star game and was cognizant of the
major disruption the fifteen-hour time difference could make on body
clocks and function. He started acclimating the team to the change
early in the week and then insisted the players stay up all night on the
flight and get on Tokyo time. I remember a Wisconsin coach whisper-
ing to me that the Michigan State players were all asleep on the plane's
upper level. "It's in the bag," he said, grinning.

I think if anything the band was helped—on both the Rose Bowl
and Tokyo trips—by the fact that we'd made a significant road trip a
year earlier, to Seattle, Washington.

The football Badgers were opening the 1992 season against the University of Washington, and members of my UW band alumni, along
with some others, helped finance and organize an effort for the marching band to go along. Our travel before going to Seattle had always
been close to home—day trips to Iowa City, West Lafayette, and the like.

That the band alumni and friends of the band would do that meant
a lot to me. Those band kids have always been like family. I was both
grateful and humbled near the end of my fifty-year career at Wisconsin
when a member of our alumni band told a journalist: "What you learn
in marching band is accountability and teamwork. You're accountable
to each other. Mike has entertained millions, but he's changed the tra-
jectory of thousands of lives by giving them an opportunity to get engaged with music."

We spent a few days in Seattle in September 1992, arriving on Thursday morning, two days before the football game. We stayed in dorms
on campus. It turned out the public affairs officer at Bremerton Naval
Base, a man named Robert Anderson, was the equipment manager for
the Badger football team in 1967. He helped arrange for the band to
play on the deck of the USS *Nimitz*.

That was something. They brought us onto the flight deck with the ship's elevator used to load airplanes. When they'd asked earlier what we needed, I said, "We don't need anything, except a lined football field, a hundred yards long and fifty-three-and-one-third yards wide. Anything else we can handle—we don't need podiums or any extra equipment."

Well, when we boarded the *Nimitz*, there was a football field outlined with duct tape—one big rectangle. They hadn't included the yard lines. I couldn't be upset—they'd done what we asked. The band improvised, and the fact is, any marching band member is used to irregular yard lines. Before there was artificial turf, I doubt there were many high school fields in the state of Wisconsin that were set correctly. Our *Nimitz* show went fine; we did forty-five minutes, and the three hundred sailors seemed to really enjoy it.

For a first venture—and as prep for our two big trips a year later—the Seattle visit was great. Following our *Nimitz* performance, we played an evening concert at the base of the Space Needle. A newspaper estimated there were a thousand people in attendance. At one point, my tuba section did what is called a skyrocket—an old band tradition of honoring someone with a brief "sss-boom-bah" salute. Skyrockets may have predated the band on the UW campus—it was a custom of students in the early days as a way of saluting favored professors at the end of a lecture. Eventually the tradition faded among the general student body, but it remained a staple of the marching band.

Out in Seattle, the tubas were honoring the city and its famous Space Needle.

Except they then called out: "Hey, Seattle, is that the Space Needle, or are you just glad to see us?"

I had to laugh. Why are the tuba players generally the rascals?

Our *Nimitz* experience was a reminder that no matter how much you prepare in advance, you must also be prepared to stay nimble and improvise.

In Tokyo a year later, the improvisation for our half-time show with Ninja was that we really didn't play at all. When I'd sent our recordings of the music to Tokyo, I'd assumed it was so Ninja could practice with it. No. When we arrived, we were told that we were to be on the field, backing up Ninja, but that we would only lip-synch a performance and our recording would play over the public-address system. It was odd, but we went with it.

Happily, the Badgers beat Michigan State 41–20, securing our first Rose Bowl appearance in thirty-one years. The trip home was one long celebration, and after boarding buses at O'Hare airport it soon became clear that much of Wisconsin was celebrating with us. People were standing at the state-line toll plaza holding welcome-home signs, and others were waving and honking their car horns all the way to Madison. It was inspiring. When the buses reached Camp Randall, the rest of the band members—remember, only seventy, mostly upperclassmen, went to Tokyo—joined us, and we played to some ten thousand Badger fans inside the stadium.

A wonderful photo ran on the front page of the December 7, 1993, *Wisconsin State Journal* that shows Al Fish, UW athletic department administrative officer, lifting me up in a bear hug that night on the Camp Randall field. What the photo couldn't convey is that when Al put me down, he leaned in and said, "Don't go anywhere afterward. We have work to do."

I think I was in Al's office until after midnight, beginning to rough out the plans for going to Pasadena. It was uncharted territory for all of us.

We did all right with it, if I may say so. Aside from a highly consequential ticket controversy that was out of the university's control—many Badger fans who were assured they had game tickets were left without—the entire Rose Bowl week was a resounding success, culminating in the Badgers' 21–16 victory over UCLA.

I was proud of the reception the band received. On January 4, the *Capital Times* editorialized about us and Rose Bowl week:

> The UW football team was at the center of attention. The athletes earned Wisconsin its berth in the Rose Bowl and they proved that they are the champs. But the band won an unofficial championship of its own. It showed the folks in California why for years at UW games, "the band always wins . . ."

Director Mike Leckrone has kept this band at top form through the good years and the lean years of UW football. It all paid off this past week. The UW band was an integral part of the spirit that made Wisconsin's trip to the Rose Bowl so much more than just a football game.

On January 1, the end of the game didn't culminate things for us. We'd secured permission to play a Fifth Quarter performance. We were running on adrenaline—a rocking half-time performance that included songs made famous by Elvis, Jerry Lee Lewis, and Chuck Berry, followed by the Badgers' victory—but the police cautioned me that if any fans tried to get onto the field, the band would be shut down. I assured them that wouldn't happen, and it didn't.

An interesting thing did happen around the Rose Bowl Fifth Quarter. Earlier, when we were just about to enter the stadium, one of my field assistants, Jim Tanner, was approached by an acquaintance of his from Wisconsin. He handed Jim a package and said, "My uncle's last request was that if Wisconsin ever made it to the Rose Bowl, I should try to have his ashes scattered on the field."

He handed the package to Jim, who was also an ordained minister, and walked away.

"I have it in my pocket," Jim told me a short time later. We were about to make that unforgettable entrance into the Rose Bowl.

"Jim," I said, "just hold on to it. We'll see what happens."

I really didn't think about it again. But later that night, Jim told me that during the Fifth Quarter, he remembered the ashes. When we were done playing, he and a couple of band members went into the Rose Bowl end zone, quietly said a few words, and dispersed the ashes.

They allowed us to use only half the field for the Fifth Quarter at the Rose Bowl. It hardly mattered. Badger fans who were surprised when we didn't play "Varsity" during the half-time show were weeping as we played it to begin the Fifth Quarter. A photo of me conducting with my hat on backward must have been taken right around that time. My smile reaches my eyes. It was one of a precious handful of what I came to call "moments of happiness" that occurred in Pasadena. Entering the stadium to the roar and the sea of red was another. From that time on, I spoke often about moments of happiness and urged my band members to recognize them as they were happening and to hold such moments close and never lose them.

I've been lucky in life, but like everyone, I've known disappointment and heartache. It's inescapable, and one reason why it's so important to preserve the good memories, the moments of happiness.

Mine start early, where life began for me—in small-town Indiana.

two

BEGINNINGS AND BUTLER

One of my most vivid early memories is marching out onto a high school gym floor and performing a baton-twirling act. I must have been six or seven. The high school band was seated in the bleachers at one end of the gym, and they played while I twirled. I don't recall much more detail—not, for instance, whether my mother had put me in a sparkling outfit (I'm guessing yes)—but there's one thing I absolutely remember.

The applause.

What's the famous proverb? As the twig is bent, so is the tree inclined.

That high school gym was in the small northwestern Indiana town of Goodland, where in summer 1941 my father, Harold Leckrone, accepted a job as a music teacher and band director at Goodland High School. I was born in my mother's parents' house in North Manchester, Indiana, on July 30, 1936. We moved often in my early childhood, from one Indiana town to another, as my dad took different band director positions. We lived in Churubusco, Monon, and then Goodland. The moves were always his choice—as a young band director he'd built a good word-of-mouth reputation.

Music was one of the great passions of my dad's life, but his pursuit of it caused a serious rift within his family. At least, I gathered as much. He never mentioned his family. Instead, I heard bits and pieces from my mom.

My dad was born in Somerset, Ohio, in 1912. Our family name, Leckrone, is likely French, though when my ancestors arrived in this country, settling in Dutch-influenced western Pennsylvania, its pronunciation soon hardened. We said "LECK-rone," accent on the first syllable. That was ingrained in me. Some in later generations—my kids among them—grew tired of correcting people who accented the second syllable. I decided long ago it wasn't a big deal and don't even notice now when it is mispronounced. My dad in a sense never had to deal with it because nearly everyone called him simply Leck, a nickname that wasn't conveyed with any disrespect—it was just what everyone called him. He didn't mind. When I once asked him why, he said, "Well, if your name was Harold, you wouldn't mind, either."

Growing up, my dad attended a strict religious school associated with the Church of the Brethren. I can't imagine that my dad's parents truly minded him playing in school bands, which he did, and quite successfully. In 1925, the Ohio State Fair debuted the All-Ohio Boys' State Fair Band, bringing together two hundred or so of the state's most talented young musicians to entertain fairgoers. All their fair performances closed with John Philip Sousa's "Stars and Stripes Forever." In 1928, my dad was selected to play cornet for the state fair boys' band, and that year Sousa attended the fair and conducted a performance of the honors group. My dad was very proud of that and mentioned it often.

But if my grandparents didn't mind Dad's school music, they almost certainly weren't happy when he began playing in clubs, performing dance music, even jazz. When it came time for college, they offered help with tuition, but only if he attended Manchester College in northern Indiana (now Manchester University), which was—and is—affiliated with the Church of the Brethren.

Even though it wasn't his choice, I think my dad liked it there. North Manchester—the name of the town—was small, but it had a lively arts scene, influenced by the college, which favored liberal arts. There was a community orchestra, which you wouldn't see in most small towns. There were swing bands, too, and my dad was in demand. He had a great ear. He could play almost anything by ear. Name a tune, tell him the key, and he could play it.

My parents met at a community function in North Manchester. Mary Louise Heeter was a local girl, and she had an eye for the talented musician onstage, who eyed her back.

My grandfather Earl Heeter was a colorful character. I was born in the North Manchester family home, and he'd often remind me that I took my first breath on his kitchen table. That house was across from the city waterworks, and my grandfather oversaw public streets and roads. He called himself North Manchester's street commissioner. I called him Grandpa. After my parents moved to North Manchester from Goodland in summer 1945, Grandpa—when I was old enough—had me up before dawn sweeping the streets. You had to do it by hand. I was probably twelve or thirteen. Nobody worried much about work permits back then.

Still, I enjoyed spending time with him. Grandpa had wonderful stories, some conceivably true, and words of wisdom he'd frequently repeat. I later used those sayings myself, including, "You can stand anything if you know when it's going to end." He said that when I was doing roadwork and he would give me a quitting time. Another was, "If it was easy, anybody could do it."

One of the legends around my grandfather was that he once knocked out the heavyweight boxing champion Jack Johnson. It happened when Johnson was on a barnstorming tour that brought him through Indiana and into a North Manchester saloon where he was overserved and unruly. Earl dropped him with one punch—I think he may have used a nightstick—and then helped get him somewhere to safely sleep it off. My grandmother, not given to exaggeration, said the story was true.

After meeting at that community event, my dad and mom started dating. One story my dad told—he had a flair for the dramatic tale himself—involved his job playing the carillon that was in the center of the Manchester College campus. Every day he'd go and play songs on those suspended bells. The administration expected religious, or at least serious, music. One day my dad alerted my mom he'd be playing a romantic song just for her, and he did, one of her favorites, "Moonlight and Roses." Unfortunately, a college official was listening, and my dad was not invited to return to the carillon.

My parents, Mary Louise and Harold "Leck" Leckrone, in the early 1950s. (Leckrone family)

My dad's Manchester College commencement was on May 26, 1933, and the following day, he and my mom were married. His first band director job was in Mentone, Indiana, beginning the series of moves that eventually landed us back in North Manchester in 1945. That year, on leaving Goodland High School, my dad received a wristwatch from the band in appreciation of his service, and my mother—who had supported them as an exemplary "band mom"—was gifted a blue-and-silver compact.

Me at age one.
(Leckrone family)

There were four of us by then. On September 24, 1938, two years after I was born, my sister, Pat, arrived. Both Pat and I inherited a love of music. She played the French horn. My parents never pushed me to play an instrument, but I caught the performance bug early—the baton twirling began in our living room before I was even school age. As I was growing up, my dad would get me started on an instrument—drums, trumpet, piano—but before long, he'd find me a private instructor. I loved playing, and on trumpet I became good early. By sixth grade in North Manchester, I was playing with the high school band. When I played with my own classmates, my dad was very strict about not acting like a prima donna. "Help them," he said. "Don't be a showoff."

About the same time—I was twelve or thirteen—my dad and I began doing a musical comedy, vaudeville-type act together. He'd play piano and I'd play trumpet, for civic groups like Rotary and Lions clubs. We had more professional gigs, too, though I never saw the money. The

I'm hoping for something bigger to ride in the future. (Leckrone family)

first money I made with music was playing "Taps" at Memorial Day services around northern Indiana. Word circulated that I was a good trumpet player. I usually received about two or three dollars for playing "Taps." My mom drove me to the services.

My dad and I often took our little show out of town. You've probably gathered by now that my dad was very musical and liked variety. He could also do musical tricks. He'd play an elaborate piano piece while wearing mittens or play with a tennis ball in his right hand. I think he'd seen Chico Marx do it. We had one bit where he'd bring his arm around my shoulder and finger my trumpet while I would bring my arm up under and finger *his* trumpet. We did it in harmony. It probably looks easier than it is, because we often had to explain to the audience what we'd done and the degree of difficulty.

I did numerous things in our show. I would sing, play trumpet (sometimes with a puppet on my playing hand), do a comedy monologue in costume, tap-dance, and play piano. In the grand finale, dressed in a grass skirt, I sang and played the ukulele to a song called

Before junior high, Dad put me in a Chester band uniform. (Leckrone family)

Dad and I had publicity pictures taken for our Vaudeville act. (Leckrone family)

"Hula-Lou." I had big rubber balls tucked under my shirt for breasts and had it rigged so that at the end I could pull a cord and one of the balls would fall out and bounce on the floor. Always classy we were not.

What we were, more than anything, was extemporaneous. He'd say, "OK, here's what we're going to do tonight." We probably had forty-five minutes of material, thirty of which we'd use at any one time. Did I enjoy it? I loved it. It should have been a tremendous father-son "bonding" experience, and, looking back, I guess it was, to an extent. But like so many men of his generation (and mine), my dad was not particularly open with his feelings, or for that matter with praise for a job well done. He might say, "That was good today." But more often, there was criticism, and he would single me out. In school band he'd say, "Trumpets, you're not phrasing that right at all. Mike, what's the problem?"

It could be he used me to diffuse the criticism of others. My dad wasn't an easy guy to know. He could be tough. But don't get me wrong. He was a lot of fun. We had some very good times.

Dad and I on stage with our act. (Leckrone family)

In Indiana in those days, most high schools had a marching band that would march at halftime at basketball games. Our school, Chester Township High School in North Manchester, had such a band, which my dad directed. I was in the band, playing trumpet, and I enjoyed it a great deal. There really wasn't anything I ever did musically that wasn't a kick, wasn't fun. Later, if there was a message I tried to convey to my students, that was it. There's a line out of a 1995 movie, *Mr. Holland's*

Opus, where Richard Dreyfuss is trying to get a kid to play the clarinet, and she can't get it. She starts crying. He says, "You know, it's supposed to be fun." That was my philosophy long before I saw the movie.

Back in high school in North Manchester, I wasn't just in the marching band—I played sports, including track, baseball, and basketball. In basketball I lettered three years and was a starter the last two. It made for a bit of a quandary. On game nights, was I on the basketball team or in the marching band? The answer is I did both. My dad needed me in the band, and my mom—who could be assertive—didn't want me to miss basketball. She wound up making me a breakaway band uniform. It had a tie and a detachable shirtfront that snapped in back. The basketball coach made sure I left the games just before halftime. I'd hustle to the band room, which was right across the hall from the gym. My mom would snap the dickey on me. I'd pull the pants over my basketball shoes, slip on a jacket, and be good to go for halftime. After the performance, it took no time to shed the uniform and be a basketball player again. It seems kind of crazy now, but we had the timing down to the second. It didn't hurt that our family was close with the basketball coach. My dad later wrote the Manchester High School fight song, which ended up being used in the movie *Hoosiers*.

I mentioned that my dad would find me private music instructors, and one of them, Larry Wiseman, was responsible for one of the truly memorable experiences of my teen years. Larry gave me trumpet lessons. His day job was as a salesman for an Indiana-based company called Conn Instruments. He was looking to have Trummy Young, a member of Louis Armstrong's band, endorse his instruments. Larry had arranged to meet the band at the Colonial Hotel in Rochester, about a half-hour drive from North Manchester, where they were performing on July 1, 1952.

He asked my dad, "Do you think Mike would like to go?"

I was a month shy of my sixteenth birthday and thrilled to go. Louis Armstrong! My only reservation—which wasn't really a reservation—was that I couldn't understand why the great Louis Armstrong would be playing a dance hall in northern Indiana on a Tuesday night.

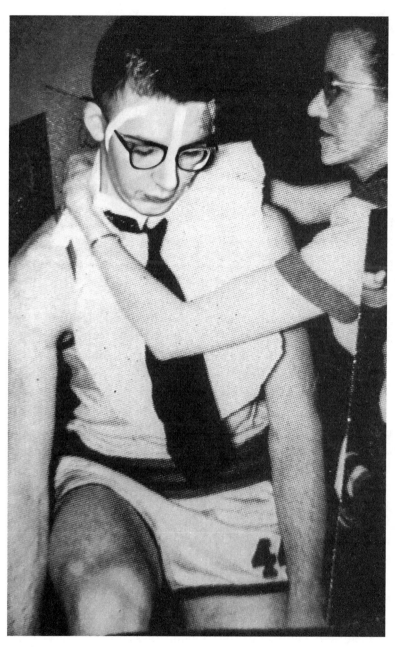

Doing the quick change for basketball halftime. (Leckrone family)

But the evening provided a major lesson for me, again something I later tried to pass on to my students. In what must have seemed like the most mundane circumstance imaginable, Armstrong gave a brilliant, energetic performance. He might have been at Carnegie Hall. I sat backstage, not ten feet away, as I couldn't be in the audience due to liquor service restrictions. Armstrong radiated enthusiasm. He opened with "Back Home Again in Indiana"—as he often did no matter where he was—and nailed it. He had a stack of white linen handkerchiefs about two-feet high, beautifully laundered, and he'd grab one and wipe his face while he kept playing. By the end of the evening, the whole stack was in a laundry basket at the side of the stage. He'd soaked through them all.

At intermission I summoned the courage to ask him—as well as the rest of the band—for an autograph. When I had my moment with him, I think I said something predictable like "I really enjoy your music." But seventy years later, I still have the autograph.

I'd noticed Armstrong applying something to his upper lip during the show, a lip that appeared severely chafed. After the show I asked one of the crew what it was Armstrong was treating it with.

"It's a substance called Tincture of Myrrh," the man said. "Louis thinks it revitalizes his lips."

I made a mental note of that and later, when I had a fever blister on my lip, I went to the drugstore and bought Tincture of Myrrh. I didn't pass that lesson on to my students. It burned to the point I thought my face was on fire.

Before seeing Armstrong, I had experienced another memorable moment with a musical giant. In fall 1950 I had the opportunity to observe an entire rehearsal and performance by the keyboard virtuoso and composer Percy Grainger. He was in town to solo with the North Manchester Civic Orchestra. As a sometime substitute (as an eighth grader!) with the orchestra, I was invited to the event. Grainger played the difficult Tchaikovsky Piano Concerto no. 1, then conducted the orchestra through a list of his own compositions.

In rehearsal and performance, Grainger was brilliant. Very demanding, but also understanding of the weaknesses of the orchestra. By his demeanor you might have thought he was working with the Chicago Symphony Orchestra. At one of his breaks, I found a few moments to speak with him, and obtained his autograph. He was very kind. Two decades later, I enjoyed another unforgettable experience when the inimitable Duke Ellington came to Madison for five days of lectures, workshops, and performances. The Duke could not have been more gracious, in situations where he could have easily been impatient, abrupt, or annoyed.

All three of those towering artists—Armstrong, Grainger, and Ellington—were terrific, when they could have understandably mailed it in. It's a lesson I have never forgotten. No matter what the circumstances, you owe the audience an energetic, exciting, unrestrained performance. I think if I had one message I hoped would resonate with all the kids I worked with, that was it.

~

One large presence in my teen years—in my life—was a girl I met in seventh grade, Phyllis Bechtold. We were born eighteen days apart. Phyllis grew up on her parents' farm outside North Manchester and attended one of the three grade schools that fed Chester Township High School and the junior high. She loved singing and music, and in fifth or sixth grade she was in a beginning band class taught by my dad. I didn't meet her until seventh grade. When I did, it wasn't the kind of moonstruck crush you sometimes hear of overtaking young people. It was better than that. We just really liked each other. We had similar interests and enjoyed being together. We gravitated toward one another. I ended up first chair trumpet in the school band and Phyllis was second chair. We'd eat lunch together and I'd walk her to the bus after school. Some days we'd go to the Dairy Bar. I think it was while we were still in junior high when one evening we saw each other at a Farm Bureau meeting. I walked her out to where the cars were parked—the adults were still inside—and that was the first time I kissed her.

By senior year in high school, I knew I wanted to ask Phyllis to marry me. Honestly, I'd known for a long time. I saved some money and bought a ring: a single diamond with two small diamonds on each side.

Phyllis and I were in the same band throughout high school. She's in the back row, second from left; I'm in the front row, third from left. (Leckrone family)

It wasn't terribly expensive, but it wasn't a trifle—Phyllis wore it for the next sixty-four years. Which, of course, tells you she said yes when I proposed on Christmas Day 1953. We were seventeen. Phyllis did hide the ring for a couple of days before swallowing hard and telling her dad, who really took it pretty well. I think everyone knew that one way or another, we were determined to be together.

We'd roughed out a plan—the first of several, as it turned out—whereby we'd go to college, not necessarily on the same campus, but close enough that we could see each other regularly. Phyllis was thinking about nearby Ball State. I had a few options with schools that were aware of my interest in music. I'd decided my future was in music. You may think that was preordained, but it wasn't. My dad had made clear I shouldn't pursue it only to follow in his footsteps. I had a real interest in chemistry and thought about chemical engineering. Having had success playing sports and having been close to my high school

Our graduation photo. By that time, I'd already asked Phyllis to marry me. (Leckrone family)

basketball coach, I felt coaching, too, was something I could be good at and enjoy. But in the end, nothing excited me, brought me joy, and brought out the best in me, the way music did and still does.

One Indiana university that was interested in me was DePauw, in Greencastle. DePauw is a prestigious liberal arts college. I was offered a Rector Scholarship, the school's oldest and preeminent academic award. It's an overall scholarship, but my interest was music, and frankly, I didn't feel the band program was on a level with the other programs at the school. I turned down the scholarship.

Second semester of my junior year in high school, a man named Nilo Hovey came through North Manchester and I had a chance to meet him. Since 1944, Hovey had been director of the concert band and chair of the Music Education Department at the Arthur Jordan Conservatory of Music at Butler University in Indianapolis. Butler was on the list of schools I was considering—my dad later earned a master's degree there—but meeting Hovey decided it. He was such a classy guy. Before Butler, he'd been a decorated high school band director in Hammond. Once I arrived at Butler, Hovey mentored me for the first few years. I also learned from Chuck Henzie, who'd been director of the Butler Marching Band since 1946. I was fortunate, early, to have men the caliber of Hovey and Henzie to learn from.

In some ways I feel I was quite mature heading off to college at Butler. I had my music goals, and Phyllis and I had our plan. She would stay in North Manchester, possibly take some college courses, but also work and save money. Eventually we'd marry. In the meantime, I'd come home often to visit.

Looking back, I may have been mature, but I was also naive that freshman year at Butler. I thought I could do it all. I did the things you do as a music student: attend class, play in the band, go to rehearsals and performances. During my student years at Butler, the Jordan music school sat nearly three miles away from the rest of the campus. It was housed in these old mansions—one had been the family home of Benjamin Harrison, a US president near the end of the nineteenth century—that weren't well maintained. You could say they had artistic charm. Someone less charitable might say they were an eyesore. And because of their location, band students often had to try to hustle a ride to a rehearsal on the main campus. It wasn't ideal.

I was also briefly out for the Butler basketball team. I'd had a successful high school basketball career and figured I could play for Butler. I found out quickly it was a big step up from Chester Township High School to the Butler Bulldogs. I might have stuck with the team, on the bench in a role as a third or fourth backup to the star freshman guard, an Indiana legend named Bobby Plump. I had been in the crowd the night he made the last-second championship-winning shot for Milan High School at the Indiana state tournament earlier that year—the shot that later inspired the movie *Hoosiers*. At Butler, I fairly quickly decided my time was better spent concentrating on music and left the team.

For a time there, however, I had all my music responsibilities, other classes, plus basketball—and I was trying to get back to North Manchester, a drive of more than two hours, whenever I could, to see Phyllis. It was unsustainable. I wasn't getting any sleep and I was a danger on the road. I was still haunted by a one-car accident I'd had a year earlier in my used 1935 Chevrolet. I was out on a country road, driving home from a date with Phyllis, when an animal jumped out in front of the car. I swerved to miss it and the car rolled down an embankment. Somehow a steel fence post pierced the car's roof, narrowly missing me. I was shaken up, but it could have been much worse. Now here I was, at Butler, a year later, fighting to stay awake driving back. That needed to change.

Phyllis and I came up with plan B: We'd get married and live together in Indianapolis. I'd get my degree while Phyllis worked and perhaps took some classes. Once I graduated and was working, she could finish her degree. Plan B wasn't our last plan, but it held for a time.

Phyllis and I were married on June 26, 1955, in North Manchester. We were both just shy of our nineteenth birthdays.

Phyllis's dad, Otto Bechtold, suggested we get in touch with a friend of his who lived in Fort Wayne and sold house trailers. He thought that would make a good starter home for us, and he was right. We found a nice trailer park that was right across from the famed Indianapolis Motor Speedway. It was called Dunne's Speedway Trailer Court. We didn't really think about it when we moved in, but a lot of racetrack people lived there. That was fun. I can recall racing legend A. J. Foyt bouncing our first daughter, Mika Jo, on his knee. More pragmatically, Phyllis began to earn money washing and ironing clothes for the racing crowd. There were times early on when we definitely needed money. I can remember being in line at the grocery store and realizing we didn't have enough cash on us to pay for everything and having to put items back. But before too long I joined a musicians' union and started to get dance band jobs. Butler also did a nice thing for me. They gave me a job in

The start of a great life together. We were not yet nineteen years old. (Leckrone family)

Our official wedding party, June 26, 1955. (Leckrone family)

what was called the special instruction division. We gave young kids music lessons. I taught trumpet to students anywhere from grade school to early high school. They paid the university, and I received a cut. At my peak I think I had fifty-five to sixty students.

~

I'd been doing well in class and learning a great deal at Butler. I had a bit of background in music theory from my dad, though nothing formal. Music theory is the study of the concepts and composition methods involved in creating music. I knew chord progression and had written some simple arrangements in high school. But my freshman year at Butler, my music theory teacher gave us daily assignments on the dos and don'ts of part writing, chord doubling, and more. She was tough—and really good for me.

She wasn't alone. I took a conducting class from Nilo Hovey, the band director. You'll recall it was meeting Hovey that convinced me I

Eating cake at our wedding reception. (Leckrone family)

should go to Butler. He had written dozens of method books for students, and taking a class from him was a privilege. He was strict—all the instructors were. Numerous students dropped or flunked out. No one coasted through the Jordan music school.

I took an introduction to music history class from Harold Johnson, an instructor who later became my master's degree advisor. He was very knowledgeable, pushed me to excel, and encouraged my interest in music history. Johnson had a specialty in the music of Finnish composer Jean Sibelius. He went to Finland in 1957 for the purpose of tracking down unknown and lesser-known music by Sibelius. In 1959, Johnson published a book on Sibelius that was regarded as definitive at the time. I became a big Sibelius fan—my master's thesis was on his Kullervo Symphony—and still have a great passion for his music.

Johnson liked me—he appreciated that I showed more of an interest than most students—and talked with me about my career choices, encouraging me to get my master's in music history and musicology. Performance—applied music—would always be there. At one point—I must have been Butler's assistant band director by then—I remember someone saying, "You're not going to be a band director all your life." Funny in hindsight—because of course I was—yet I never regretted my immersion in music history and musicology.

I graduated with cum laude honors from Butler in June 1958. A month earlier, I was named to the Butler chapter of Phi Kappa Phi, a prestigious scholastic honor society. The initiation was held at a banquet on May 16 at the Atherton Center on campus.

I had decided on graduate school, studying music history. One day in my senior year, the marching band director, Chuck Henzie, called me in and said, "I'm going to start hiring a graduate assistant."

He hoped I'd be interested, and I was. It was a three-year assistantship during which I would also be working toward my master's degree. Phyllis and I had moved out of the trailer into a two-bedroom cement slab house on Brittany Road. We liked Indianapolis, and in some ways it still felt like a small town. We were happy there.

With Charles Henzie, my boss at Butler. (Leckrone family)

My graduate assistant role included writing the arrangements for the Butler marching band. To a musician, arranging means you are taking a basic melody and giving it some individualized treatment so a band or orchestra could play it.

Henzie did the show charting for the band's performances at Butler football games, figuring out the marching on the field. He and I worked well together. Before the first football season of my assistantship, we met at his house with the Butler band announcer and a few friendly band alumni to plan the shows. Those planning days were enjoyable, almost like a party. Once the shows were planned, I wrote the arrangements. I found I had a talent for it. During my time at Butler the band played only my arrangements.

I was busy during graduate school, partly out of necessity. Phyllis and I had our second child, Kristopher Alan, born in 1958, and I was trying to earn additional money. These days you might say I had some side hustles. I worked with high school bands during summers and breaks. Schools were interested in having guest conductors come in and show their students a different approach. I enjoyed that and did a lot of it.

As time went on, I also kept playing professionally—many, many freelance trumpet gigs. I liked doing it and would be less than honest if I didn't admit I occasionally thought about trying to play trumpet for a living. I didn't, of course, but I learned a lot playing those jobs. Indianapolis had a vibrant live-music scene. I eventually played regularly with the Indianapolis Concert Band, and performed as well—freelance work—at everything from charity balls to rodeos. They'd call and ask if I was available. My range of musical interests worked to my advantage. I could play with a symphony or with a combo in a dive joint. Whatever the job, I felt like I could handle what they wanted.

The groups I jobbed with played country club dances, and for a time we had a regular Saturday night gig at the Fort Benjamin Harrison non-commissioned officers' club. One of our most unusual venues was a club on North Meridian Street called the Rat Fink Lounge. My marching band members later had trouble believing there was a club in Indianapolis with that name, but there was, and I played there. What proved to be our last night at the Rat Fink came when a patron threw lighter fluid on our piano player's keyboard, followed by a match. Gene, the piano player, moved away from the flames and shouted, "That's it. We're out of here!" And we were. I can't remember if we were paid.

One time I was called to back up pop singer Jack Jones at an Indianapolis nightclub show. I was in the band room with the other musicians right before the performance when Jones walked in and said, "You know, guys, I'm having a little trouble with my throat tonight. I'd like you to play the show down a half step." That was challenging—the entire performance in a slightly lower pitch. But it was a great experience. For those gigs, we rarely rehearsed the music for a show all the way through. We'd do spot rehearsals. It was good for learning how to fly by the seat of your pants. And the fact was, if you didn't stay on your toes, the next time a job came around, you didn't get a call.

Before my graduate assistantship was finished, the head of the music school called me in and said a music theory professor was taking a leave of absence for a year and Chuck Henzie had recommended they hire me as a theory instructor. It was to be a one-year faculty position, and at the same time I would keep doing the things I had been doing with the marching band. I jumped at it. My plate was full—overflowing—but I was either too dumb to know it or smart enough to sense that showing up when asked with energy and enthusiasm would pay dividends.

At one point during that second year, the theory instructor I was temporarily replacing decided not to return to Butler, and I was asked to stay on. It proved a pivotal moment in my career. I said yes. It was the only full-time job I had before coming to Wisconsin.

I was "assistant band director" but that title hardly covered it. Jack-of-all-trades is a cliché, but I felt like one at Butler, doing so many different things musically. I arranged the music for six or seven ballets during my years there. Butler had a first-class dance school, primarily ballet—classic, modern, and jazz. They knew I liked all kinds of music and had the arranging ability. We'd sit down and the choreographer would map out how many measures or how much time they wanted. It was challenging and allowed me to be creative, because while they were supervising everything, I made a lot of decisions on the style and content.

I worked with the drama department at Butler as well. One of their projects brought together a mix of professional and student actors for a performance of Bertolt Brecht's *Mother Courage and Her Children*. It was a strange production—Brecht is kind of out-there no matter how you look at it. At that performance, I conducted the Butler University Brass Ensemble—twenty-six musicians plus piano and accordion. A Chicago actress named Viola Berwick played Mother Courage.

The Brecht play was at Lilly Hall on the Butler campus. You'll recall that during my undergraduate time the music department was housed a few miles from the rest of the campus. In 1962, a year before the Brecht play, Butler had opened Lilly Hall, the new home of the music school. It was on the campus proper and made the lives of all music students and faculty easier. I was invited to solo on the hall's opening night and was pleased to read in the next day's *Indianapolis News* that "the trumpet piece, with Michael Leckrone as soloist, was delightful."

That same year the *Indianapolis News* carried a story that was somewhat less pleasing to read, at least until everything could be explained.

The headline read "Students Go to Jail for Dear Old Butler."

The story behind that headline starts with the Butler men's basketball team making the NCAA tournament—before it was called March Madness—and then upsetting Bowling Green, 56–55, in a thrilling first-round game at Lexington, Kentucky. It meant the Bulldogs were into the regional semifinal, played that year in Iowa City. The Bowling Green game was on a Monday and Butler's game against Kentucky in Iowa City was just a few nights later. Things moved quickly. It was decided I would take fifteen members of the band to Iowa City to perform during the game. We rode a commercial bus. Before we left, Chuck Henzie told me he would arrange accommodations by phone while we were traveling. It really was all last minute.

When we exited the bus in Iowa City and I called Henzie, there was an ominous silence on his end of the phone.

"You'll have to get back to me," he said, or something to that effect.

It developed that there were no hotel rooms to be found in Iowa City. Of course not! The NCAA regionals were in town.

The band played at the game—Butler lost to powerful Kentucky by twenty-one points—and when we called back to Indianapolis, we still had no place to stay. What to do? We were walking the streets with our instruments when I spotted the police station and courthouse. Inside, the officer in charge was sympathetic and said we could sleep on benches in and outside the building's courtrooms, and there were also some empty jail cells we were welcome to use.

It was a long way from the Ritz, but we managed some sleep and made it through the night. In those days there was a third-place consolation game, and we played that afternoon as Butler beat Western Kentucky, 87–86 in overtime.

It would have all been fine except for that newspaper headline the following Monday. One of the kids must have talked to the reporter. Chuck Henzie received a call from the university president. Jail? I was called in to explain, which I did, and it blew over, as it should have.

~

We were always looking for ways to get the band some positive recognition. In 1963, we released a long-play, monaural recording titled *Butler Bowl Ballads*. It included pop songs like "Mack the Knife," selections from the popular Broadway show *West Side Story*, and the fight songs from several Indiana universities—DePauw, Evansville, Notre Dame, Indiana, Purdue, and of course Butler. The lyrics of "Butler War Song" begin: "We'll sing the Butler war song / We'll give a fighting cry / We'll fight the Butler battle / Bulldogs ever do or die."

I still have a copy of that LP. It was pretty advanced for its time; not many college marching bands were putting out record albums. (Butler released a second marching-band album in 1977.) We were just happy that our project paid for itself. We'd had to scrape together funds with help from the Butler Alumni Office to finance it.

We'd built the band to around 150 members by the time we did the album. They were an interesting mix of young people. I wasn't that much older than many of them. We had some Korean War veterans. Decades later, when I returned to Butler for an alumni gathering, I was still directing the Wisconsin band, but some students who had been in my early Butler bands were already retired.

My experience is that marching band members enjoy playing occasional pranks, and my early Butler bands were no exception. One year we were asked to march in an ROTC parade in Indianapolis. Nobody really wanted to put on Butler band uniforms and march in what was in effect a military parade. I agreed to do it but had the band wear ROTC uniforms instead. Since nobody wanted to do it, I picked band members who'd had attendance issues or other minor problems—it was a way for them to erase those demerits.

For the drum major I picked a guy who'd been in ROTC, a nice enough young man but a bit self-important. This was not lost on his fellow band members. I was walking alongside and could feel something stirring.

The parade route went up Market Street into Monument Circle in downtown Indianapolis, continued partway around the circle, and then turned off onto Meridian Street. Well, my band had conspired to not make the turn onto Meridian. They kept going around the circle. The drum major, of course, was in front and had already turned. He wound up marching by himself down Meridian. It looked like a scene from *The Blues Brothers*.

~

I've mentioned how much freelance work I did while I was at Butler—teaching high school bands and playing trumpet professionally. Another thing I often did was help people who thought they had an original tune but couldn't put music on paper. They'd come in with a tape-recorded version or just sing it live right in front of me, and I would transcribe it for them. No great masterpieces resulted, but it provided some much-needed additional income.

I also wrote half-time shows for many high school bands in Indiana, and by the mid-1960s I'd written several arrangements for George Vaught, the band director at Anderson High School. Their band had a rich history in marching band competitions.

During that time, George served as music instructor and band director for the Indiana State Penitentiary at Pendleton. One summer, George called and asked if I could fill in for him in that role for a couple of weeks. I've always been receptive to offers that bring a new experience, and I had no reservations about saying yes to George. I will say I had an uncomfortable feeling when those big steel doors slammed shut behind me, and I was inside.

As it turned out, it was fun to work with the inmates. For them it was a welcome break from the routine of prison life. It allowed some of them to be creative. There were no disciplinary problems—any bad behavior would result in loss of privileges. For the most part, they were interested in my musical experiences and expressed regret that they hadn't taken advantage of musical opportunities they'd had along the way.

There were a few times when I had the chance to introduce the band to an audience. I always said, "Ladies and gentlemen, the Pendleton State Prison Band, and their theme song, 'Time on My Hands.'"

In 1967, a man named Fred Ebbs asked me to help with part of the half-time show for the 1968 Rose Bowl game between Indiana University and the University of Southern California. Ebbs was the new director of the marching band at Indiana, the famous Marching Hundred. I'd first met Ebbs when he was directing the Hawkeye Marching Band at the University of Iowa. Having done some freelance show writing for him, I continued when he took the job in Bloomington. Ebbs would call, give me the name of a tune, and say, "I want so many measures here, so many there," and so on. I'd write it and take it to the post office and mail it off. Sometimes, not often, he'd call and ask for a change.

The 1968 Rose Bowl was Indiana University's first time in the Rose Bowl—and they haven't been back—so it figured that Ebbs would put together an Indiana-centric show for the Marching Hundred. He called it "Adventures in Hoosierland." I wrote a portion of it. One tune the Marching Hundred played was an arrangement of "Stardust," a song written by Bloomington native Hoagy Carmichael. Carmichael is said to have written "Stardust" at a campus hangout called The Book Nook in 1927. In his autobiography he saluted The Book Nook, which in 1931 had a name change to The Gables: "Its dim lights, its scarred walls, its marked up booths, and unsteady tables made campus history."

They also played "76 Trombones," from *The Music Man*. While an Indiana native didn't write "76 Trombones," it fit in IU's show as a tribute to Elkhart, Indiana, which was home to enough instrument manufacturers that the city called itself the band instrument capital of the world. In Pasadena the Indiana band played it while in formation shaped as a trumpet.

The half-time show went better for the Hoosiers than the football game, which they lost to USC by the score of 14–3. The player of the game? The Trojans' O. J. Simpson.

By the time of that Rose Bowl, I'd been promoted to director of the marching band at Butler. It happened in 1966 and it felt like a natural progression—graduate assistant to assistant director to director. There was a feeling among some people on campus that I was insisting I get the job or I'd leave. That was never the case. I wasn't averse to looking at other opportunities—and I did, more to gauge the market than anything else—but Chuck Henzie and I had a good-enough relationship that we could talk through and defuse any turf battle before it began. We had lunch together several days a week after rehearsal and had discussed how he would probably pass the marching-band top job to me one day. On one level, that understanding let him occasionally give me more work, which I'm sure he didn't mind. He taught percussion and conducting, and I think that by 1966 he'd reached the point where he felt he should step away from the marching band, which can be very demanding. There was no search committee or anything like that in those days to fill the job. I was positioned for it, and the university basically asked me if I wanted it—which I did.

Something I instituted once I became director at Butler was a precursor to the varsity band spring shows that later became so popular in Madison. I did them for three years at Butler in Clowes Hall, the big auditorium that opened on campus in 1963. We called the performances

I ended my Butler years as director of the marching band. (Leckrone family)

"Highlights and Blackouts." I assembled a varsity band out of my marching band members. They performed with a women's dance group called the Butler Color Guard, more popularly known as the Half-Time Honeys. We played Broadway show music and other popular tunes and sold tickets at a nominal price. We included a few other acts in the performances. Most memorable was the time I asked a local trumpet player named Jim Edison—an excellent musician—to impersonate Al Hirt, the famous New Orleans trumpeter. He was built like Hirt—more than pleasingly plump—and we put a fake beard on him. The audience bought it, at least for a little while. Those nights were fun.

Another of my fond Butler memories was getting to work alongside a remarkable character and true Bulldog legend: Paul D. "Tony" Hinkle. He served as head football, basketball, and baseball coach at Butler and was athletic director at various times. An amazing record! Is it any wonder the fieldhouse at Butler is named Hinkle Fieldhouse?

Whenever I went to Tony's office with a question or concern, he was gracious and easy to talk to, though I was never sure if he knew my name. I was always "kid," which is what he called everybody.

The band director job was demanding, but I kept up my ancillary activities once I had the top job. One example: In March 1968, I conducted the select band—seventy of the top musicians from five high schools—at the Hancock County Band Festival. I was heavily involved with high school bands throughout my time at Butler.

I judged high school band contests on both a county and state level, and I wrote marching shows for numerous schools, including their state fair performances. I arranged the state fair shows for Richmond High School five consecutive summers, and in 1968 they honored me at halftime of their homecoming football game. Several of my band members at Butler had come from Richmond, including a young man named Steve Varnell, who then returned to Richmond High School and was assistant band director (to John Parshall) when they honored me. Steve became the school's band director in 1977. I was introduced before that 1968 game and conducted "The Star-Spangled Banner." I'd written the half-time show, and the band's first formation took the shape of an *M* and an *L*. It was very nice—kind of a cherry on top of all the work I had done with high school bands in Indiana over the past decade.

That fall of 1968 also included a memorable half-time show at the Butler Bowl, where the football Bulldogs played their home games. I was proud of the shows we'd done since I became director. Butler played only four or five home games a year, so we had time to prepare the shows.

Even while I was assistant director, the band had been pestering me to do a patriotic show. I'd always resisted, feeling it was kind of a cheap way to get applause. The audience is compelled to like it. But the kids kept after me. In fall 1968, I acquiesced, with a caveat. I said if we were going to do a patriotic show, we'd pull out all the stops and make it a patriotic performance that could never be topped or repeated.

One side of the Butler Bowl was completely free of spectator seating, so I was able to use a huge American flag as a backdrop for the show. We had a men's chorus, equipped with microphones, on the sideline. Our last song would be "The Battle Hymn of the Republic." We had one hundred Boy Scouts who would all carry American flags onto the field.

There was more, including pyrotechnics. Finally, I'd arranged to have five hundred pigeons released near the conclusion. The fellow who had the pigeons told me they would fly out of their cages, likely circle in the air above the field, and then fly home—they were homing pigeons.

The day of the show, everything clicked. The big flag unfurled perfectly, not touching the ground. The crowd loved it when the Boy Scouts came out. The men's chorus sounded great.

I gave the cue for the pigeons to go, which they did, and then a few seconds later I signaled for the fireworks. Nothing happened. I cued the pyro guy again. Still nothing. The show ended and I went down, somewhat upset, to see what happened.

He was apologetic, and said, "I pushed the fire button, but in the delay between the dress rehearsal and the performance we must have lost a connection someplace."

I shrugged. I wasn't happy but stuff happens.

"But Mike," he continued, "it's a good thing. I pushed the buttons to fire and if they'd fired when they were supposed to, the way those pigeons flew they would have been directly in the line of fire. It could have been ugly."

Once the band members heard that story, they never let me forget it. A half century later they still talk about it.

That was memorable, but it was another half-time show in that fall of 1968 that played a role in my making a significant career move—not the performance itself but a rehearsal for a Butler half-time show.

I received a phone call from H. Robert Reynolds, who in spring 1968 was named director of bands at the University of Wisconsin. I'd talked with Reynolds then about the marching band job in Madison, but he'd pulled back, deciding he wanted to get settled in the job before making any permanent personnel decisions. I was disappointed and wondered if he wasn't just using that reasoning to brush me off.

Apparently not, because some months later, in fall 1968, he called wanting to come and watch me rehearse with the Butler Marching Band. He brought an eminent UW professor of clarinet, Glenn Bowen, with him.

Was I nervous rehearsing the band in front of them? Honestly, I was not. I had a show to get ready. It didn't really matter who was watching. In a way, I forgot they were there.

It must have gone OK. Two or three days later, Reynolds called from Wisconsin. Could I come to Madison for a formal interview?

I sensed my life was about to change.

three

WISCONSIN

I liked Butler and enjoyed my time there very much. I've said I could have spent my entire working life in Indianapolis and not been unhappy. While that's true, a music career, like any other job, doesn't happen in a vacuum. I'd seen what other Midwest marching bands were doing. I felt we'd built the Butler band into something that was equal—if not superior—to bands I'd observed at Purdue, Indiana University, and other bigger campuses. It made me a little restless, wanting to see what else might be out there for me. I was not without ambition, and Phyllis was encouraging when I talked about looking elsewhere. Obviously, a pay bump wouldn't be a bad thing, either.

I interviewed at Western Kentucky University in Bowling Green, and at the end of the day they offered me the job. I said I'd get back to them because I wanted to talk to my wife, which was true. After Phyllis and I discussed it, we decided Indianapolis was likely better culturally, for both us and our kids, than southern Kentucky.

The job I interviewed for and really hoped to get was at the University of Minnesota. The interview went well, and I received a call saying I was a finalist (they didn't say how many finalists there were). I was hopeful. Their program was going through some changes. I'd oversee the marching band but not be director of bands. It would have been a good fit for me, but I didn't get the job, which was a disappointment.

I was initially concerned Wisconsin might be another one.

The University of Wisconsin had a storied band program that dated to 1885. In 1934, a man named Ray Dvorak, who'd been assistant band director at the University of Illinois, was hired to lead the Wisconsin bands.

Dvorak established an exceptional marching band shortly after his arrival in Madison and is credited with many performance innovations at football halftimes. The University of Wisconsin news service once noted of Dvorak, "He developed the singing band, mass singing, formations without signals, and animated formations. He originated the airplane band formation with sound effects; the formation of the score of the game immediately after the game; flank and oblique movements in formations; and the playing of 'salute' songs to the competitors."

Ray is also credited with adding the arm wave to the time-honored Badger song "Varsity."

In 1948, Ray Dvorak was asked to judge the Tri-State Music Festival in Oklahoma. The train ride there changed his life. Fourteen miles from its destination in Enid, Dvorak's train was smashed by a heavy truck, an accident that killed two aboard the train and left more than forty injured. Dvorak's injuries were among the most serious. He was badly burned and his right arm was amputated.

Yet his quotes in the news stories immediately following the crash were a testament to Ray's indomitable spirit.

He vowed to return to lead the Wisconsin bands and said, "Music is not interpreted with the hand. It is interpreted with the heart and mind; and expression comes out no matter how it is portrayed physically."

Dvorak nevertheless insisted that his prosthetic right arm be formed with a fist so he could put a baton in it. He became an inspiration to many and a formidable leader in the nascent disability rights movement in Wisconsin.

I came to know Ray Dvorak a little bit in the 1960s at a Midwest band clinic he hosted annually in Chicago. There was no question who was in charge. If a band was playing and some others were chatting or otherwise not paying proper respect, Dvorak would call them out.

"How would you like it if somebody was talking while *your* band was trying to play on stage?"

It took some people by surprise in 1967 when Dvorak announced he'd be retiring from the Wisconsin job the following year. The position was posted, and I sent in an application. I didn't get an interview. But then a few things happened. At the end of the 1968 spring semester, Jim Christensen, who had been assistant director of bands and effectively director of the marching band under Dvorak, resigned to take a lucrative position as director of music at Disneyland. Around the same time, Bob Reynolds was hired as UW's director of bands. He was a University of Michigan graduate, a French horn player, and on the faculty of California State College, Long Beach, when he was hired at Wisconsin.

In Camp Randall Stadium with H. Robert Reynolds, the man who hired me to come to the University of Wisconsin. (UW Bands archive)

Reynolds, needing a marching band director, called me cold in Indianapolis. I assume he'd seen the application I'd sent earlier. That he'd found enough in it to call me I took as a positive sign. Could I, he asked, have an informal meeting with him in Chicago to talk about the UW Marching Band position?

Reynolds and I met at the famed Conrad Hilton Hotel near Grant Park in Chicago. We sat in easy chairs in the spacious lobby and had a nice conversation. Weeks later, the streets outside the hotel would be the scene of a riot between Chicago police and antiwar protesters during the Democratic National Convention.

Reynolds was pleasant but cautious that day. It was a positive conversation, but he stopped short of making an offer, saying they would get back to me.

When they did, a few days later, it was to say the department had decided to hold off on hiring a full-time marching band director. Reynolds wanted some time to assess how things stood and check out the situation further before making a key hiring decision. He asked a former graduate assistant, John Gates, to direct the marching band on a one-year, temporary basis. In retrospect, that seems reasonable, but at the time I took it to mean Wisconsin didn't want me.

That fall, as I've noted, Reynolds was back in touch and came to Indianapolis to watch me rehearse the Butler band. Then they invited me to Madison for a formal interview in front of the executive committee of the School of Music—all the full professors. It was my first time in Madison and the visit was a success. I think Reynolds had let it be known—perhaps not in so many words—that I was the guy he wanted. The interview was almost perfunctory. What was my vision for the marching band, and so on.

I was given a hard hat and a tour of the new Humanities Building at University Avenue and Park Street on campus, which was getting close to its fall 1969 opening. It housed the School of Music and Mills Hall, the premier performance space on campus.

I met Dale Gilbert, chair of the School of Music. Dale was a terrific guy. His son, Jay Gilbert, played in my UW Marching Band in the 1970s and went on to a distinguished career in music, retiring in April 2022 as director of instrumental music at Doane University in Nebraska.

The most amusing part of the visit to Madison was my required interview with a dean in the College of Letters and Science, home of the music department. This gentleman sat on the edge of his desk and swung his legs up and down while we chatted, like it was Howdy Doody time. Our conversation was not memorable, but it was pleasant.

At the end of the day, Bob Reynolds drove me around the campus, and we wound up at the top of Observatory Drive, with its glorious view of Lake Mendota.

"We're going to offer you the job," Bob said. "Will you take it?"

I said yes.

"We'll have the paperwork to you next week."

Before my official start date in June 1969, I took Phyllis up to see the city and look for a place to live. I think she was excited for me but a bit wary of a new adventure. She'd never lived outside Indiana and, of course, had a small-town upbringing. Butler University, where we'd spent the last decade, was in those days a conservative school, almost a church school, having been chartered in the nineteenth century as North Western Christian University. I wore a necktie almost all the time I was at Butler. The women wore nice dresses.

There was no one to chaperone Phyllis and me on her first visit to Madison. We walked around the campus and up State Street. She didn't say much and I kept thinking that it was a long way from North Manchester. The guys had long hair. Windows were boarded up in the aftermath of antiwar demonstrations, and angry graffiti covered walls and doors.

Starting our drive back to Indiana, when we were about at Madison's city limits, I asked Phyllis what she thought of our new home.

She cried until we reached Rockford.

～

To Phyllis's credit, she adapted quickly and was well occupied at home. Our third child, Milissa Kay, had been born on the day after Christmas 1967 (ever since, she's felt slighted having her birthday so close to that big gift-giving occasion), and our third daughter, Milinda Kae, was born on Phyllis's birthday, July 12, during our first Madison summer. For my part, I was too busy to worry much about culture shock. I was teaching three or more classes, which was a sign of the times. Everyone seemed to teach more in those days. My classes included arranging and wind band, which was essentially a history of the wind band. Bob Reynolds had established a new group on campus, the Wind Ensemble, using members from the Symphonic Band, which was itself newly renamed from the Concert Band. I also taught a music appreciation course, which was designed for nonmusic majors and later turned into a popular class that both the students and I enjoyed very much.

For all that teaching, my primary challenge was resurrecting the marching band, which was in a fallow period by 1969. I was the third different director in the past three years. It wasn't stated overtly, but within the School of Music the marching band was regarded as a second-class enterprise compared to the rest of the school. That was not unique to Wisconsin, but it was a hurdle to get over, as was the completely dismal performance of the Badger football team on the field. They had failed to win a game in either the 1967 or 1968 season. Not a single victory! Attendance faded and the enthusiasm in Camp Randall Stadium went with it.

Much of that was outside of my control. What was in my control was how hard I could work and what kind of example—and expectations— I could set for the kids.

By August of my first summer in Madison I had a list of the leaders—seniors and otherwise—from the 1968 marching band. I invited them to my house for a cookout and I spoke about my hopes for the coming year. I was blunt.

"I don't think the work ethic of this band is what I want it to be," I said. "I am going to expect a lot more effort than what I think has been happening."

Meanwhile I was trying to push the numbers up. The figure that sticks in my mind as our final tally is ninety-six, which was very small for a Big Ten marching band. And to get ninety-six I went everywhere. I tried to enlist people I'd already convinced to be in the band to call their buddies.

We drilled hard that first preseason, emphasizing physical conditioning. There was some early grumbling among the band, and a story has
endured that a lottery was established in which some members bet on
how long I'd last. Instead, the grumblers left. My first band wasn't very
good—let me be honest—but they had great spirit and tried hard. I
looked for things that could help them develop pride. The first one was
a move called "Horns Up," in which they quickly elevated their instruments in a snapping motion. They began to take pride in it, and I can
remember telling them they might have room for improvement elsewhere, but they were going to have the best damned "Horns Up" in the
country. We went from there to working on the marching step, insti-
tuting a high step in which the musician's knee hesitates while lifted
at forty-five degrees. We called it "Stop at the Top."

That phrase—which I coined—was a descriptor of the step we fash-
ioned out of the high stepping that all Big Ten marching bands utilized
in those days. It was called the "Big Ten style" for many years. I thought
the step could be made more energetic by having them hesitate once
they've brought their foot up, toe pointed down, rather than have it all
be a continuous fluid motion. It's not a float or a glide. You put more
energy into bringing the foot up than putting it down.

"Stop at the Top" became a kind of catchphrase for bringing the
energy to every performance. It became part of the UW Marching
Band vernacular. I should note that it is anything but easy to teach and
to do. My first year or two, we had the Big Ten style down pretty well,
but what took a while longer was the stop. It was something I felt I
could never let up on.

I may not have articulated it plainly, but at the core of what I was
getting at was the idea that hard work and fun need not be mutually
exclusive. Putting in the time and effort to excel at a performance and
then pulling it off bring tremendous satisfaction—and it's fun.

I'd always felt we were entertainers. From the outset I wanted variety
and I wanted the shows to move quickly. The goal was to achieve the
best of both worlds: a combination of good, interesting music with
plenty of marching snap and style.

I told the band—and I said this when doing clinics as well—that when you're doing a show, you must do it so that two different people in your audience get equal enjoyment from the performance: an audience member who is blind and an audience member who is deaf. In other words, you need to excel both visually and musically. Now, those two people perhaps won't get the maximum possible enjoyment, but you've given it the best you can for them.

~

At Camp Randall football games, the half-time show is the marching band's showcase. But the pregame performance is important too. When I came to Wisconsin, people were asking me, "How are you going to do the run-on?" I wasn't sure what they were talking about. I found out the run-on was true to its name. Twenty minutes before the opening kickoff, the band runs out of an end-zone tunnel onto the field.

It was supposed to be organized but it was more haphazard. My first idea with the run-on didn't help. I had the band come out of three tunnels instead of one, to speed things up, which it did, but it also caused them to lose communication, and we had guys running into each other. We went back to one tunnel after the first game.

What I wanted to do with the run-on was a bit like constructing a story. I wanted to build anticipation. I had the tubas come out first, a little slowly, followed by the drums. People by then are anticipating the music. Then the rest of the band runs on. I stressed the importance of staying in step—looking organized!—and part of that was always keeping one foot on the ground, which you don't do when you truly are running. Up to my last rehearsal decades later, we were still schooling the freshmen on keeping one foot in contact with the ground.

Our pregame show opened with a fanfare to announce the band— "Da-Dadada-Da-Dadada"—but it was far too long at the beginning. I shortened it, and then went into "On, Wisconsin!," though I shortened that too. "On, Wisconsin!" has three strains to it, though the first two are really not well known any longer. But Ray Dvorak liked them. I had us stop playing the first two strains and instead go right into the "On,

Wisconsin!" everyone knew as the band began marching down the field. The crowd always roared, but some people weren't happy. They thought I was messing with tradition. Ray never objected, even though I know he was very fond of the first two strains. I did play them when we started our Field House concerts. If anyone objected at the football games, I could say we played the whole song at the Field House.

After we played "On, Wisconsin!," I had us play the opposing team's school song. Next was a catchy tune, often a popular song of the day. We'd close with a patriotic song—perhaps "God Bless America"—and then, of course, "The Star-Spangled Banner." Eventually, for our exit, I added "If You Want to Be a Badger," a song everyone knows and likes and claps along to. If you want to accuse me of manipulating the audience, I plead guilty.

Our first half-time show of the 1969 season was a tribute to Elroy "Crazylegs" Hirsch for Wisconsin's home opener against highly regarded Oklahoma. That the Badgers played a respectable game (losing 48–21) was an omen. Hirsch had arrived on the Madison campus as athletic director six months before I came to town. He had been a Badger sports hero, and there was a sense that he could help turn the football fortunes around. He did. In the fourth game of the season, the Badgers beat Iowa at Camp Randall, the team's first win in three seasons, and the city went crazy in response. Hirsch led the charge to State Street to celebrate.

I really hit it off with Elroy. We both ran on adrenaline and enthusiasm. We saw humor in situations others took far too seriously. One example: Early during our time in Madison—the year was 1971—some Camp Randall fans in seats close to ground level complained to Elroy about the tuba march that occurred between the third and fourth quarters. They called it a distraction. The march was a ritual in which the band's tuba players walked and played in the area between the field and the stadium seats. After some kids began throwing wads of paper into the tuba bells, the band was given colorful red covers for their instruments and enjoyed showing them off during the tuba march.

Most fans loved it, but in October 1971, Elroy briefly acquiesced to the complainers and asked us to stop the tuba march. That in turn

Elroy Hirsch—here playing the tuba at the band banquet—was someone I enjoyed spending time with when he was director of athletics at UW. We had a great mutual respect. (UW Bands archive)

sparked a counterprotest, with many more people demanding the tuba march return. One day at lunch in the Kollege Klub I was asked to sign a petition to bring back the tubas. And then at the November 6 Homecoming game against Purdue, half a dozen or so alumni band members grabbed tubas and defiantly marched and played. The crowd loved it, and Elroy, who had always kind of shaken his head in a "what is it with some people" way about the complainers, rescinded his order. Then, to show there were no hard feelings, Elroy stopped in at our end-of-season band banquet and marched around playing the tuba, poorly!

As I said, we were friends. If I stopped by the athletic department suite of offices and he spotted me, Elroy would wave me into his office for a chat. At one point he even told me that he'd been contacted by the Los Angeles Rams—where he had been a top executive before coming to Wisconsin—about returning to the team with a promotion. If that happened, Elroy asked, would I be interested in joining the Rams as music director? I didn't hear about it again and Elroy stayed in Madison, but I was flattered and think it speaks to the kind of relationship we had.

The football season of 1969 had an auspicious ending. As Phyllis and I settled into our new life in Madison, things were going reasonably well, but it was an adjustment, no question, maybe more so for Phyllis than me. We were looking for signs we had made the right move.

My wife was a big believer in omens. If she saw a monarch butterfly, for instance, she believed the next day or two were likely to be great. Our last home game that first year was in November against Illinois. I'd planned a Christmas-themed half-time show. Just as the band went into formation as a Christmas tree and began playing "White Christmas," it began to snow. I have to say the timing was incredible. And when I saw Phyllis afterward, she gave me a big smile and said, "It's going to be OK."

~

In my first year at UW, we also established a band for athletic events. It was part of my charge when I was offered the job in Madison. They wanted me to shape up what was then called the basketball pep band, a somewhat disorganized, ragtag group, with haphazard instrumentation—

not a good situation. It had been suggested we make participating in it a condition of being in the marching band, but I didn't like the idea of it being conscripted and forced on anyone. I wanted it to be fun, and once we had it organized and could set a schedule, it caught on with the kids. I came up with the name—the UW Varsity Band—because I thought "pep band" lacked class and Wisconsin had its signature "Varsity" song. Why not use it for the name for the athletic band?

One thing that helped the varsity band take off was an assist from the Badger basketball booster club. I'd spoken at one of its meetings and talked about trying to establish an identity for the band that played at the games at the Field House. The booster club purchased somewhere between thirty and forty red-and-white-striped jackets for the band to wear over white shirts. I think the varsity band was a hit right off the top. If you have three dozen musicians in red-and-white jackets sitting courtside behind one basket, you have an immediate presence.

My second year, 1970, we increased the marching band numbers to almost 150. We also took a road trip that proved pivotal in my effort to turn around the marching band culture at Wisconsin.

The varsity band at the Field House, showing off their candy stripes. (UW Bands archive)

The road trips the band had made since I'd been in Madison were limited to day trips to places like Evanston and Iowa City. In October 1970 we went to Indiana University and stayed overnight. As you can imagine, it was an important trip for me, going back to my home state with my new band.

The Badgers were playing the Hoosiers in Bloomington on October 24. Indianapolis had more and better hotels, so our plan was to stay there Friday night and drive down to Bloomington early Saturday, where we would rehearse before the game. The band was excited about this first overnight trip, and—alas—took full advantage of being away from home. They stayed up late partying, losing sight of the reason for the trip, which was the performance they'd be giving Saturday afternoon. On one level, I almost understood it—Wisconsin's football fortunes had been so bleak that among some fans the partying at the stadium trumped the games in importance—but that was changing under Elroy and new head football coach John Jardine. We needed the band's value set to change with it.

I could tell there were a dismaying number of blurry eyes and blurry brains on the bus ride to Bloomington. Once we began rehearsing, my worst fears were confirmed. They didn't have it. They were missing turns and running into each other. Twenty minutes in, I threw up my hands.

"That's it," I said. "I can't watch this anymore."

I walked away.

I think they were stunned. Rehearsal time is precious, and they knew this show meant a lot to me. I've heard since that in the two hours between that abortive rehearsal and the start of the game, there were several conversations about pride and responsibility. That soul searching paid off. They gave a great performance at halftime—by some accounts the Indiana fans gave the band a standing ovation. It set a tone for us going forward. The Badgers won the game, too, 30–12.

~

I think many of the people who enjoyed our marching band performances at Camp Randall would have been surprised at how much work was involved to make them a success. In the 1971 season—my third year in Madison—we practiced for two hours, from midafternoon to late afternoon, at least four days a week on the recreational fields on the west end of campus. In monsoon rains we would occasionally go inside the nearby Stock Pavilion, but that was rare. Over time a saying evolved within the band. Question: "What do you do when it rains?" Answer: "Get wet."

A reporter who observed us the week before Wisconsin's 1971 Homecoming game against Purdue started his story by quoting my instructions during one practice:

"Hit it!

"Lean on it!

"Come on, get those knees up!

"You people are going to diddle around until Friday, and we're going to be out here until dark practicing. Now let's go through that formation one more time!"

I could get a little animated.

But we were better in that third season. My drum major, Ray Luick from Madison West High School, had been with me all three years—a field captain who really held the band together. He'd been a tuba player as a freshman but embraced the drum major role, returning often over the years to be drum major with our alumni band.

When I arrived in Madison, I'd arranged to have UW Extension film our half-time shows. I would watch the film of Saturday's performance by myself on Monday. Then I would watch it again with my assistants, and finally we would go through it several times with the band. I kept telling them that little mistakes can kill a show. A knee that's not high enough or someone moving in a lazy shuffle—the cumulative effect is a perception of a lackluster performance. We began making note on the band bulletin board of the mistakes in each show—and we identified the musicians who committed them. That sheet of paper soon had a name: the Dummy List.

Around that same time, the band initiated an annual award that has endured for decades. It was named for Karl Strieby, a French horn

player who was a sophomore my second year as marching band director. The Strieby Award was given to the band member who during
the season makes a mistake with the greatest amount of class. One of
my mantras was, if you're going to make a mistake, don't do it by being
careful. If you're going to make a mistake, go after it. Karl—who, I
should add, was a good player—set the bar for this in a game in the
1970 season.

During our half-time show we were playing "Basin Street Blues," a
number popularized by Louis Armstrong and others. I'd arranged for
the band to be in formation in the outline of a trombone, and the routine was fairly simple: the guys who were part of the trombone slide
would march out and come back sixteen steps, mimicking the motion
of the instrument. Karl Strieby happened to be the end musician on the
slide. At that point in the show, those in the slide, including Karl, went
out sixteen steps, and came back sixteen steps. But the second time the
slide went out, for some reason Karl went out only eight steps, and
turned. The rest of the slide musicians went out sixteen steps, turned,
came back, and rejoined Karl, who handled it marvelously. There was
no indication that he'd messed up. He acted like it was part of the plan.

After the game, another band director who was in attendance came
up to me and said, "Mike, good show. But I have to ask. That thing
with the trombone? I didn't get what you were doing." He couldn't
believe a kid had made that major a mistake. I began calling errors done
with style and authority "Striebys." A few years later, when Karl returned
to the band as a field assistant, the flugelhorn section suggested that an
annual award and trophy be presented to the band member who best
combined an error with a touch of class. The Strieby Award was born,
which I'm not sure Karl appreciated.

In 1971, less than 10 percent of the band—which totaled 161 musicians—were students from the School of Music, and around 40 percent
were from the College of Engineering. Engineering students know how
to work hard with a goal in mind. A longtime dean of engineering at
UW–Madison, John Bollinger, was a talented trumpet player and as a

teen was awarded a full scholarship at the Juilliard School of Music. We had a couple of conversations about the engineering–marching band synergy, and John noted that the typical engineer (or budding engineer) personality likes a chance to be productive even when not actively engaged in an engineering project. Marching band filled that bill.

I had been lobbying for new band uniforms and more road trips, but budgets were still tight—though we'd get new uniforms the following year. Our road trip that 1971 season was to Evanston for the Northwestern game. Five weeks later, we played our Homecoming show at Camp Randall. The Badgers were up against Purdue. At home games then, our schedule involved a 9 a.m. first rehearsal of our half-time performance at the stadium. I described the Homecoming show as "a nostalgic look backward through modern eyes," and I'd written arrangements for "Try to Remember," from the off-Broadway musical *The Fantasticks*, and "Proud Mary." After the game—which the Badgers won 14–10— we marched to the UW Children's Hospital and played a twenty-five-minute concert. It capped a long day of marching and playing, but the look on those young faces always made it worthwhile. The hospital stop had been a meaningful band tradition for decades.

By 1971 the varsity band had begun playing at Badger ice hockey games as well. At the time, nobody would have dared dream how significant— even legendary—the band–ice hockey association would become. That it happened at all is due to the exuberance and persistence of Bob Johnson, who came from Colorado College to coach hockey in 1966. Johnson was so colorful and his personality so infectious that he had two nicknames: Badger Bob and the Hawk.

When Johnson saw the varsity band at a basketball game, bedecked in their red-and-white-striped jackets, he immediately knew they could make an impact on the crowd at home hockey games, which were being played in the plush, new Dane County Coliseum.

Johnson began pestering me. "We need to have a band at the hockey games," he'd say.

My standard reply was, "We're not quite ready to do that." The truth was, I was leery of assuming another responsibility, a further time commitment. Hockey is a long season. But Johnson wouldn't let it go. He was insistent. I think at some point we both realized I was going to cave; it was just a matter of when. Finally, I agreed we would do an occasional hockey game, one night of the two-game weekend series.

Bob soon said, "We need you more."

I next agreed that the band would play at every Saturday night game. He could get high school bands for Friday night. But the Friday night ticketholders started complaining they weren't getting the UW band, which was an immediate hit in the rowdy, beer-drinking atmosphere of the coliseum. I finally gave in completely, agreeing to do both nights. Part of that decision was the atmosphere—the band kids were having fun.

The ambience at the coliseum was truly special. The band would arrive on a bus in time to be ready to play a half hour before the opening face-off. By the time we showed up, the place was packed, and it's likely that some of the fans weren't on their first beers. Since the band was seated near the Badgers' bench, Johnson would call on us when he felt the team needed a boost. He'd make eye contact with me and shout, "Come on, Leckrone! The crowd's dead! Get them going!" It was never adversarial. It was Bob Johnson being Bob Johnson.

Along with being a charismatic character, Johnson was a terrific hockey coach. He took the Badgers to the finals of the NCAA hockey tournament—what is now called the Frozen Four—in March 1972. It was held at the Boston Garden, and I know some members of our band really hoped we could make that trip. But the only road visits we'd been making were to away football games. The Badgers lost in the 1972 semi-finals, 4–1 to Boston University, but then beat Denver 5–2 in the third-place game.

The next year, when the Badgers again made the Frozen Four and I mentioned to athletic director Elroy Hirsch how great it would be if the band could go—it was again at Boston Garden—he surprised me by saying yes. This was March 1973. I think Bob Johnson had something to do with our getting to go.

The following anecdote may give you an idea of how fired up Madison had become about Badger hockey. In late February, during the run-up to the postseason tournament, the Badgers played a series at Notre

Dame. The first game was Friday, February 23. That day my wife, Phyllis, went into labor with our son Erik. I was in the delivery room that evening as her labor progressed, and her doctor and I had the hockey game on the radio from South Bend. I'll never forget that when the game ended, the doctor turned to my wife and said, "OK, Phyllis, the game is over. You can have the baby." And she did.

The band took a bus to Boston for the 1973 NCAA semifinals and final. Our hotel wasn't fancy—to say the least—but it was near Boston Garden and the band had a great time. UW fans showed up in droves. Their enthusiasm was remarked on by the national press and would soon become legendary. A *Sports Illustrated* writer noted there were some thirty handmade signs and nearly all were pro-Wisconsin, including this: "On Boston ice the embattled Badgers swirled, and fired the shot heard round the world."

I don't recall if it was displayed in Boston, but one favorite sign of Badger fans during that era read "Jesus Saves, and Talafous Scores on the Rebound." It referenced Dean Talafous, a stellar skater from Hastings, Minnesota. Talafous would play a key role as the action in Boston unfolded.

Wisconsin played Cornell in the semifinals, and the Badgers had a very slow start. Cornell scored forty seconds into the game and went up by 4–0 in the second period. *Sports Illustrated* wrote later that "not even the world's most implacable cheering section seemed to be doing any good." The Badgers were getting a lot of good shots on goal, but as the writer noted, "They hit every inch of the Cornell goalie, his pads and his stick."

Elroy Hirsch must have sensed the same thing. The band was seated in the balcony, and I recall Elroy coming in during that second period and telling me, "We just need to lose our virginity!" He meant that once we scored one goal, the spout might open. Elroy had a funny way of viewing the game. The athletic director became too nervous to watch for long. He'd come in and briefly talk to me, then go back and pace the arena hallways.

With the Badgers down 5–2 and about thirteen minutes left in the third period, we played "You've Said It All," the polka-like song made popular in Budweiser commercials. We'd first played it earlier that season at the coliseum, and it had quickly caught on as a fan favorite, with "Wis-con-sin" inserted in place of Budweiser at the end. Now when we played it in Boston, Gary Winchester scored for the Badgers to cut the Cornell lead to 5–3. Our fans went crazy, but then time began to slip away. With about four minutes remaining—please don't hold me to these exact time sequences, but it's as I remember it—we again launched into "You've Said It All." And then Jim Johnston scored for the Badgers! Now it was 5–4. The seconds were ticking. Cornell kept clearing the puck out of its defensive zone, content to play keep-away. Under a minute to go. Desperate, the Badgers forced the puck into the Cornell zone. With eighteen seconds left, a Badgers shot hit the Cornell goalpost. So close! Cornell tried to clear but the Badgers' Dennis Olmstead grabbed the puck and passed it to Dean Talafous near the goal. Talafous shot—and scored! The Badgers had come back from 4–0 and 5–2 to tie the game. There were five seconds left.

In the overtime, Talafous scored again—on a rebound!—to secure the breathtaking 6–5 victory for the Badgers. My recollection is that the band played "You've Said It All" repeatedly into the night. We didn't want that feeling to end. It was magical, the start of the song becoming iconic for us, and fifty years on, it endures.

Two days later, the Badgers beat Denver, 4–2, to win their first NCAA hockey championship. Sports Illustrated's story on the weekend concluded with a final paragraph that saluted the band: "The Badgers were the new rulers of the collegiate ice. A band of redcoats played 'On Wisconsin.' Outdoors it was St. Patrick's Night, and Boston was on the verge of changing colors."

There would be other championships, and even a Frozen Four in Providence in 1978 when the Badgers didn't win the title, but the fans and band were such a hit that the Providence Chamber of Commerce later presented UW with a plaque celebrating their enthusiasm. That was the tournament when a story circulated that Elroy Hirsch put $500 down on a Providence bar and said anyone wearing red could have an Old Style on him. The tale was recounted to me so often I tend to believe it, and knowing Elroy, it wouldn't have been out of character. For all that, however, the first national championship in Boston—given the circumstances—still resonates most with many longtime Badger hockey fans.

Those fans and their conduct—I'll include the band here—largely received accolades through the years, as the Providence chamber award makes clear. Not everyone loved them, of course. The chanting of "*Sieve*" at opposing goaltenders was seen by some as lacking sportsmanship. In a game at the coliseum against Colorado College, early in that first championship season, the band took exception to a call that went against the Badgers and began chanting, "The ref is out to lunch! The ref is out to lunch! Eat it, ref—raw, raw, raw!" One of the referees skated over to the public address announcer, Phil Mendel—who developed his own mystique with Badger fans—and told Phil to tell me that if it happened again, he'd eject the entire band.

It rarely reached that level of animus. The only truly regretful moment I recall happened at a game two years later, when the Badgers were playing the University of Minnesota Duluth at the coliseum. A Bulldog player, Tom Milani, was upset enough at the taunting from fans that when he and his teammates came onto the ice after a period break, Milani skated by the band along the boards, raised his stick, and took down a row of trombones. It was like a picket fence collapsing. About half the slides were damaged to the extent they no longer worked. The Duluth contingent was apologetic and paid us to repair the instruments. I don't know that Milani was being malicious. I think he saw them sticking out from the boards and couldn't help himself. Milani ended his career as a Bulldog with one hundred goals and a place in the UMD hockey hall of fame. His citation does not mention either Madison or trombones.

Truth is, where referees were concerned, I likely found myself in more hot water at basketball games at the Field House. Early in my time in Madison, the Big Ten basketball referees were not as professional as they became later. There were some games when the calls were wildly erratic. One came in January 1976, when the Badgers were playing at

home against Minnesota. The Gophers' star center played most of
the second half with four fouls and never fouled out, even though, in
the words of Wisconsin coach John Powless later, "he ran over three
players right on the court." Three technical fouls were called on the
Badgers. One of the three referees, Rollo Vallem, who lived in Madison,
told me later they realized they'd called a poor game. With ten seconds
to go and Minnesota up by double figures, I led the band in "Three
Blind Mice." The crowd loved it. Powless did too. He stood up on the
bench and rallied the fans, waving his sport coat over his head. Then
he came over near the band and helped conduct "Three Blind Mice."
Somehow that didn't draw a technical.

⁓

The band liked to have fun, and that included on road trips when we
stayed in hotels. I'd say 99 percent of it was harmless, and I was usually
alerted and asked to stop the mischief.

Once when we were staying in the Bismarck Hotel in Chicago, the
phone rang in my room.

"Mr. Leckrone," a voice said, "you need to come downstairs. One of
your students is riding on our elevator."

I didn't get it, and said, "Well, what's the problem?"

"You don't understand. He's not riding *in* the elevator. He's riding
on the elevator." He'd pushed open the ceiling of the elevator and was
sitting on top with his legs dangling down.

Another time, in Ann Arbor after a game against Michigan, I heard
some late night or early morning rustling at my door. Sometimes I
didn't go to bed at all on those nights. I wanted the kids to know I was
around. That night, I clearly hadn't patrolled the halls because when I
heard the rustling and opened my hotel room door, the doorway was
bricked up with stacks of Gideon bibles.

I'll share just one more. This was in Bloomington, at the hotel after
an Indiana game. One of my assistants knocked on my door and said,
"Mike, you need to come into the men's room."

I've noted we had a lot of engineers in the band. When I went into the hotel restroom, it developed they had unscrewed and relocated the partitions separating the row of toilets. All that was left were the bare toilets.

I found the likely perpetrators and said, "Funny, guys. I'll be back in an hour and those partitions will be back up."

They were.

four

NEW VENTURES

People may be surprised to learn that the marching band's first performance at a professional football game was not at Lambeau Field, home of the Green Bay Packers.

In early 1974, I received a call from Rudy Custer, who was a Madison native, a UW–Madison alumnus, and business manager of the Chicago Bears for thirty-eight years. Rudy wondered if the UW band might want to come to Soldier Field that fall and entertain when the Bears hosted the Packers.

It turned out to be an important event for us. It went exactly the way I thought it would. The game was October 21, 1974. When we were introduced, the Chicago crowd booed. Of course they did. They associated us with the Packers. But after our half-time show, the crowd gave us a standing ovation. For me it ranked as a significant performance, a turnaround moment similar to the Indiana road trip a few years earlier. We'd given a big-time show at a big-time venue and turned around an indifferent audience.

It would be another fifteen years before we first played Lambeau. That was October 1989, and the Packers were hosting the Dallas Cowboys. The sports editor of the *Stevens Point Journal*, Don Friday, wrote a column two days after that performance in which he remarked on the festive atmosphere at Lambeau:

Give a major assist to the jazzy University of Wisconsin–Madison marching band. Nobody can entertain a football audience better than veteran director Mike Leckrone and his 200-plus member outfit. In the last few years, as a matter of fact, about the only highlight for fans attending Badger home football at Camp Randall was watching the pregame, half-time and post-game performances by the nationally-acclaimed band. At least 80 percent of the sellout throng of 55,656 fans stayed glued to their seats for the band's 30-minute post-game show which soon had the stadium rocking and rolling. Now that's entertainment.

The Packers' public relations director, Lee Remmel, told the *Wisconsin State Journal* he'd received numerous calls on the Monday following the game asking when the band might again play at Lambeau.

Why did it take until 1989 for the band to play at Lambeau? I don't think Ray Dvorak was interested in playing at a professional sports event, and then, too, the Packers had their own band for a time. After the Packers' band broke up, I spoke with the team about taking our band to Green Bay. My hope was that in return the team might make a donation to Very Special Arts Wisconsin, a terrific organization I was involved with that provided arts programming for children and adults with disabilities.

The Packers graciously agreed to make a $5,000 donation to VSA Wisconsin, and Wisconsin Bell offered to underwrite the band's travel expenses to Green Bay. As those newspaper reports indicate, the band was a big hit at Lambeau. But the papers didn't mention the funniest thing that happened that day.

Early in the week the tuba players had been saying they really hoped they could do a march-around at Lambeau. I checked with the Packers, who said they were fine with it. So at the end of the third quarter of that game against Dallas, my tuba players began their march. I watched and as they marched past each section of spectators, the fans rose in a standing ovation. The tuba march generally received a lot of love from the stands, but this was extraordinary. It was almost like "the wave," the rolling stand-and-extend-your-arms stunt that sports audiences later embraced. I'm not sure the wave had made it to Lambeau yet.

So why were the fans standing and cheering? I found out when the tuba players turned and came past where I was seated. They had taken masking tape, or something similar, and put a letter of the alphabet on all the tuba bell covers. Their marching formation spelled out THE BEARS STILL SUCK.

It was hilarious, but still, I made kind of a halfhearted attempt, later, to reprimand them. It was a popular phrase and sentiment in Wisconsin, though the language was a little crude for that time. But I wasn't really mad. Then I took a phone call from my dean, who wasn't truly angry, either, but said, "Just remind the kids that they're highly visible and representing the university."

The story's coda came a short while later at an event at the residence of UW–Madison's new chancellor, Donna Shalala, a savvy New Yorker who recognized from the outset the abundant goodwill Badger athletics and the marching band generate for the UW.

A pompous and humorless individual in attendance approached Shalala and mentioned the band's Lambeau appearance. Halftime was fine, this gentleman allowed, but did the chancellor know what the tubas did?

"They spelled out 'the bears still suck,'" he said.

"Well," Shalala said, "they do, don't they?"

～

By the time of our Soldier Field performance in fall 1974, the band was two years into wearing new uniforms that I'd had a hand in designing.

The uniforms I'd inherited when I arrived in 1969 dated to around 1960 and were red and black and rather military looking. They had a long coat without much decoration. I think that was partly because Ray Dvorak had wanted a uniform he could use for both his concert group and the marching band. The problem with that is you wind up with a uniform not really designed for either, and one that lacks personality.

I knew we needed to modernize them, but it wasn't until 1972, when Bob Rennebohm, executive director of the University of Wisconsin

Foundation, led a $25,000 fundraising effort, that we were able to purchase new uniforms. Early that year I flew to Wichita, Kansas, and spent two days working on a new look with designers from Fruhauf Uniforms Inc., the country's preeminent band uniform manufacturer.

I had some ideas about what I wanted. For starters, I didn't want stripes on the pants. If the musicians aren't lifting their legs to the same height, the stripes accentuate that—it's a bad optic. I also wanted the pants—once we tailored them—to rest about five inches off the ground. You'll see bands with pants that are baggy and dragging on the ground. It's not a good look. We also didn't design belt loops on the pants. We use suspenders with a very high waistband, which means that when someone lifts an instrument, you don't see the shirt underneath. I originally wanted black pants, but the Fruhauf designers recommended instead a very dark blue. You can't tell it's not black until you put black next to it. The dark blue is much richer. And no pockets, which the kids didn't like and still don't, fifty years later. We did give them one back pocket for a wallet. If it bulged, the coattail would cover it.

The front of the coat was shorter than previously, waist length, wide shoulder, narrow waist. In my first design, the front was reversible. After Fruhauf produced uniforms with this design, the side we used most of the time was red with a black W emblem; the emblem on the reverse side was red with a white border. We hardly used the red emblem because, given the uniform's white back, it didn't emphasize a turn. You needed that color differential. It also grew dirty fast. We moved away from the reversible coats after Fruhauf pointed out that they were considerably more expensive and needlessly so if we weren't using the other side.

The emblem itself evolved, after the university sponsored a contest to create a new logo for the school. I thought one of the contest entries—white inside red, with each color forming its own W—would be a great logo for the university. When it wasn't chosen, I grabbed it for the band uniform. It has been highly popular, but you can always count on someone finding fault. One gentleman took to calling me repeatedly, asking why the UW band was promoting the Jewish religion. He thought it

looked like a menorah. I was polite but finally suggested he call the dean
of students—who happened to be Jewish—if he wanted to comment
further. One call concluded that discussion.

I was more inclined to agree with a designer at Fruhauf in Wichita
who pointed out that the emblem resembled a lyre, which is a stringed
instrument in the manner of a small, U-shaped harp. Our emblem could
be seen as a symbol of music. I liked that.

I wanted the hat to be white, with a red-and-white plume on top.
And I wanted decoration. We used a lot of sparkling silver, which I felt
was a classy look. There's a chain above the visor, which I liked immediately when Fruhauf recommended it. I designed the medallion in the
middle, a multisided starburst with a plain W.

For a time, our shoes weren't uniform. That is, band members wore
their own black shoes, which we then enhanced with white spats that
covered the ankle and instep and disguised the fact the shoes weren't
alike. Eventually the athletic department—once Camp Randall Stadium
had artificial turf—bought us football cleats, because they felt we were
leaving marks on the turf with our repeated steps in flat shoes. The cleats
gave us a more uniform look.

Along with the new uniforms, the UW Foundation fundraising campaign helped us buy sixteen new sousaphones. A sousaphone is sometimes called a marching tuba—and we generally referred to our players
as the "tuba section"—but a sousaphone is slightly different in that it
coils around the player with the bell pointing forward. The sousaphones
when I arrived in Madison were mostly white and fiberglass and didn't
have a good sound. The few brass sousaphones were painted white to
appear alike, but I thought it caused the tuba section to detract from
the whole appearance of the band. The tuba section is highly visible. We
needed new instruments and were able to get them, which was great.

The band played the new sousaphones and wore the new uniforms in
public for the opening home game of the 1972 season, when the Badgers played Northern Illinois. It was "band day," a tradition begun by
Ray Dvorak a decade or so earlier, when selling tickets to the games was
a priority. UW could charge a dollar a ticket, and some three thousand

In Camp Randall, we spent a lot of time working on spacing, and I think it shows in this photo. (UW Bands archive)

students from roughly forty Wisconsin high school bands would come and sit with their instruments in the lower stands. At some point Ray—and later I—would conduct as they played three or four songs. The band day experience lessened as the Badger teams on the field played better. Selling vastly reduced-price tickets was no longer beneficial, which I understood.

At their best, the band days were good for us as a recruiting tool. I made a point of encouraging my newest band members—many of whom had been at high school band day the year before—to go up into the stands and tell everybody what a great experience they'd been having with the UW band.

I laughed and said, "Lie about the director."

But it worked. Throughout my career, many band kids would come up to me and say, "My first experience was when I saw you at high school band day and I thought, 'Boy, I want to be a part of that!'"

$\sim$

A change of some significance occurred with the band in 1974. During my years at Butler, women were in the marching band. The Big Ten conference, however, had a policy through the 1960s that marching bands be male. It was tradition. Most of the marching band members came out of what was then the all-male ROTC—military training that was mandated in the charter of land grant universities.

By the early 1970s, of course, things were changing, sometimes grudgingly. There were lawsuits at some Big Ten schools. At Michigan State, when women were declared eligible for the marching band for the first time in 1972, a Lansing newspaperman spoke with the assistant band director.

"We had a feeling this would happen," he said. "So, last year, we conducted a little opinion poll."

The paper reported the results: "Out of 215 [male] marching band members, 210 said they opposed opening up the ranks to coeds."

I will give myself and UW credit for a more enlightened attitude. I knew it was inevitable that women would be joining college marching bands. And I knew from Butler that all the things guys might say—that women couldn't physically bear up under the marching and so on— was baloney. They did just fine at Butler. So we took out the male requirement for the marching band at UW–Madison in 1971.

It wasn't widely publicized, and when we began to get inquiries from women, I sensed they were looking for a door to knock down—a door that in our case had already been opened.

More than once I took a call from a woman who said, "What do you have to do to be in marching band?"

"Show up," I said.

And they never did. I think they were looking for a political fight. Even though we'd opened the ranks to women in 1971, it was 1974 when the first two signed up. Their names were MaryAnne Thurber and Paula Schultz, and they were absolutely the best we could have hoped for. They didn't shy away from being called pioneers, but they weren't making a cultural or political statement. Marching band is highly demanding, and if you stick, it's because you want to march and play.

I spoke with both Paula and MaryAnne during registration week in fall 1974. I met with all the new kids one-on-one. I had them play for me. Paula played trumpet and MaryAnne played saxophone. It wasn't easy for them in the beginning. They took some ribbing—the first pants they were given had like a size-fifty waist—but the thing is, *all* the new members did. We stressed unity and camaraderie, and they fit in pretty quickly. They never complained. They just did their thing. MaryAnne later became one of the first female officers with the Madison Police Department. And Paula, well, she ended up working for the National Security Agency. If you asked for more detail she'd laugh and say, "I could tell you, but then I'd have to kill you."

In 1975, the number of women in the band increased to fifteen. It grew to twenty-one in 1976, thirty in 1977, and kept climbing. By 2003, the split was roughly 60–40, with women nearly equaling the number of men. Over the years they've brought all kinds of positives to the band, but one for certain was their willingness to be less reserved, to be less stoic than the guys. If you feel good about playing, let everybody know! They did. Another positive: the band's average grade point went up.

~

In March 1975, Bob Reynolds, the man who hired me to come to Madison, announced he was stepping away as director of bands at UW. It wasn't a complete surprise because he was leaving to return to the University of Michigan, where he'd earned both his undergraduate and master's degrees.

Bob and I had an excellent relationship. Part of my feeling that way, I suppose, is that he let me do my thing and didn't interfere with what I was doing with the marching band. He'd come to the football games, and occasionally he'd make a suggestion, which was always welcome. But he never said, "You need to do this" or "that." Bob's leaving had a greater impact on the concert groups, because he was so popular and well respected in that arena. He initiated the Wind Ensemble program at UW.

With Bob's departure I ended up with the title of director of bands. There was a feeling among some in the School of Music that I'd insisted on getting that title—that otherwise I would consider leaving. That was not the case at all. What I was concerned about—and spoke of to Bob and others—was that they not bring in someone for the position who might want to tell me how to direct the marching band. In the end, it wasn't even really a formal hiring process. They more or less just asked me, "Would you like to be director of bands?" I said yes. It was more titular than anything, although I did take on some additional administrative tasks.

The School of Music hired a young man named Eugene Corporon to be director of the Wind Ensemble. He'd studied conducting with Bob Reynolds and they had a good relationship. Gene and I were fine together, and he, understandably, didn't have much to do with the marching band. He had his own thing. He currently is a professor of music at the University of North Texas, where he conducts the Wind Symphony.

~

The same month that Reynolds's departure was announced—March 1975—we played a varsity band concert at Mills Hall in the Humanities Building that included many if not most of the members of the marching band. I'd been thinking about a fitting climax to the band season, something akin to the spring "Highlights and Blackouts" shows I initiated once I became director of bands at Butler. Something that would bring all the kids together one more time before the school year's end. Our annual band banquet was in the fall after football.

I thought about it and spoke with some of the kids, who, predictably, said, "Let's have a party!"

I said, "Let's have one last performance." I told them we'd come together at Mills Hall, put on one last show—play some favorites from the past year—and after an hour and a half or so of that we'd go have our party. That seemed to satisfy everybody.

I mentioned that we always needed a few extra bucks for uniform or instrument repair, so I thought we'd charge $1.50 for people to attend the show.

One band member, Mark Blaskey, scoffed. "There's no way," he said, "that anyone is going to come and pay $1.50 to see this band."

Well, the concert received a bit of preshow publicity—small stories in the *Wisconsin State Journal* and *Capital Times*—and we were pleasantly surprised when between 450 and 500 people came to Mills Hall. It was a fun—if bare bones—show. Our production values consisted of turning on the lights. But the energy was there. I was wearing a red blazer, and by intermission I had completely soaked through it. The only change of clothes I had was a really loud red-white-and-blue shirt. When I walked on wearing it, a few band members hooted and hollered. That began my tradition of always trying to top myself with glitzier suits at the spring concerts.

It was that kind of night—the atmosphere loose and enthusiastic. Afterward, people were asking if we'd do another one next year. The band was already asking me what I might wear. My friend Phil Mendel, the hockey announcer, was adamant that we make it an annual event.

The second year, Mills Hall was overflowing. All the seats were taken and people were sitting in the aisles. A fire marshal who was in attendance estimated the crowd at nine hundred, which was about a hundred more than capacity. He didn't do anything that evening but told me afterward that we needed a bigger venue.

In 1977, we moved to the Field House. Again we weren't long on production values. There was no money to build a stage, so we put the band on the basketball floor and the crowd—twenty-eight hundred that year—in the west bleachers. I sent the band staff out to various high schools to borrow lighting and anything that might be used for a stage production. We found floodlights, a sound system from Good'nLoud Music, and kind of pieced together a production. I'm sure we violated numerous building codes.

The varsity band concerts were enormous fun, and the word spread. Before long theater professionals were volunteering to help with the staging. We went to two nights in 1988 and three nights in 1994. We began to have guest musicians and vocalists, Madison legends like Doc DeHaven, Little Vito and the Torpedoes, and harmonica virtuoso "Westside Andy"

Linderman. In 1993, my School of Music colleague Richard Davis joined us. Richard, one of the world's preeminent bassists, had played with everyone from Sarah Vaughn to Dizzy Gillespie (and later Bruce Springsteen).

In 1998, we moved the shows to the Kohl Center. It reminded me of something a few years earlier when we'd introduced pyrotechnics into the varsity band concerts. (There was very little we didn't do, including suspending me on wires so I could fly through the air.) When we began the pyro at the Field House, our athletic director at the time, I think it was Pat Richter, chuckled and said, "Maybe you could burn the place down." They were looking for a new facility by then. Beloved by some, the Field House by 1990 was outmoded. One year we did accidentally catch an NCAA boxing championship banner on fire and had to replace it. Another time my hair was singed.

The three-night extravaganza in April 1998 at the sparkling new Kohl Center drew this review from the *Wisconsin State Journal*: "There was

Moving into the Kohl Center gave us a whole new set of opportunities for special effects. (Gary Smith)

confetti, a blimp, fireworks, strobes, flags and everything from Broadway musicals to a Fifth Quarter Chicken Dance."

It was all a long way from essentially passing the hat at Mills Hall, and it grew bigger and better still over the next two decades.

Mentioning the chicken dance—a silly polka move that became a regular part of our shows—puts me in mind of a unique individual who first drew public attention in the fall of the year of our first varsity band concert.

It was at a home football game at Camp Randall in 1975 when a man named Terry Westegard, frustrated with another pending Badger loss and fortified with just enough Cold Duck champagne, slipped down from his seat in Section X, grabbed some spare pom-poms, and joined the ranks of the tuba section and the pom-pom squad as they made their way around the oblong track that circled between the football field and the stadium seating.

As Westegard told the *Wisconsin State Journal* the following year, "I got swept up by the beat of their cheer and just had to join in."

The fans—especially those in his home Section X—roared their approval. Within a game or two later, Westegard had donned a Bucky T-shirt, red cloth helmet, and furry red skirt.

The roars grew louder. In November 1976, following a home game against Iowa, the Sunday *Wisconsin State Journal* bestowed celebrity status—and a new nickname—on Westegard, with a page 1 article and a photo headlined "Plumber Partial to Pompons."

Reporter Dick Jaeger's story began: "Why does a portly Portage plumber pose as a pompon person?"

With that, the Portage Plumber entered Camp Randall Stadium lore.

His timing was perfect. The football team was good enough that they weren't an embarrassment that kept fans from coming (as in two winless seasons in the late '60s), but neither were they so good that those fans couldn't use some fun diversion. Our band benefited from this circumstance as well. Fans loved the music and the marching, and if the team lost, well, they could live with that—the stadium scene was a happening. For a few years the Portage Plumber was a part of it.

Terry Westegard, aka the Portage Plumber, added even more fun to the Camp Randall experience.
(UW Bands archive)

A lot of people thought I might have objected to the attention Terry was getting as the Portage Plumber. That wasn't the case. Terry and I were very friendly. First of all, he was a great guy. He was actually rather shy, once you knew him. It made it a little strange that he would get out there and do what he did.

I think some of the band, at first, regarded him as an intruder. I know the pom-pom girls definitely did, early on. But he became such a part of the show. If he'd been a jerk I'd probably have felt differently. He was just so nice.

Terry came to me at one point and said, "If you don't like me doing this, just let me know." Instead, we incorporated him into our act, at least on one occasion. We had a bit that started very solemnly. We had a coffin or something resembling a coffin, and suddenly it popped open and out sprang the Portage Plumber. Years later, when I tried to explain the phenomenon to people—members of my band—who had never seen him, they couldn't really understand it. Terry signed autographs, made personal appearances—once he even appeared at a UW football recruiting banquet in Milwaukee and received a standing ovation. For a time, the Portage Plumber was part of the magic of Camp Randall.

The time, in retrospect, was relatively brief. Terry stopped his act midseason in 1981. He later told a magazine writer that it had lost its luster for him.

"It was like I looked up into the stands after my final performance and thought, 'This is it,'" he said. "I just did it like I always did, and the moment went away."

~

In the latter half of the 1970s, I continued working with high school bands beyond our annual band day at Camp Randall. In June 1976, I was one of twelve music educators named to the board of advisors for the first national high school championships of Marching Bands of America. The event brought together outstanding high school bands from across the country for a competition that was held at the University of Wisconsin–Whitewater. Along with judging the competition, the advisors taught classes for both students and instructors.

I looked at it as a win-win. I was able to meet some of the giants in the band industry as part of that board and became friends with them. For another thing, the University of Wisconsin paid attention to how you grew your CV—curriculum vitae, which is essentially a summary of your career. For promotions, you had to submit your CV to the personnel committee. They never pushed me to get a doctorate, but it was important to enhance my CV. Serving on boards was one way to do it. I started as an assistant professor and was promoted to associate and then finally full professor at UW.

Another thing I did with high schools was involve them when the marching band was making a road trip with the Badger football team.

On many trips, we'd make a deal with a school to do something in their community the night before a Saturday game—perhaps play during a Friday night high school game. In return, the band would get lodging. Sometimes people with big houses would take in as many as eight band members. The kids enjoyed it because they were treated like royalty and ate great meals, dinner and breakfast. It helped me from a budget standpoint, and it was good public relations.

On a trip to play Michigan State in October 1978, we performed the night before at halftime of the game between the Dexter High School Dreadnaughts and the Novi High Wildcats. The Dexter band director, Gerald Woolfolk, had played in my band at Butler and sent me a letter asking if we'd be interested in performing.

As I said, it was good public relations. The *Detroit Free Press* did a big story on our appearance in Dexter and quoted a local woman saying, "Everybody is talking about this. Something like this has never happened here before. People in town who don't even have kids are coming to the game."

Earlier in 1978, I traveled to Europe as a member of an unusual Madison musical group called the Original Hyperion Oriental Fox Trot Orchestra. The band was formed in 1974 by Rick Mackie, who was a UW grad student at the time (and later executive director of the Madison Symphony Orchestra), and Karlos Moser, longtime head of University Opera. Rick was from New Orleans and had access to a whole catalog of great 1920s and early '30s jazz-age music at Tulane University. Rick knew that cornetist Bix Beiderbecke was one of my musical heroes and invited me to play with the band, which I did and very much enjoyed. We played Beiderbecke's "Riverboat Shuffle" and a lot of other things that were in his style.

The Hyperion Orchestra's trip to Switzerland in May 1978 was under the auspices of the Madison chapter of the Friendship Force, which had arranged an exchange of visits with a European chapter.

When we landed in Zurich, the idea was to have everybody disembark and gather in a large room where we'd pick up our luggage and meet the local residents who had volunteered to house us.

The room in Zurich was certainly large—it was a discotheque. They started calling people's names and connecting them with the residents to whom they were assigned. Everybody's name was called—except mine. The hall was emptying out. I finally went up to the man in charge and provided the name of the resident I was going to stay with.

"Oh, he died," the man said, matter-of-factly.

I was told he had a fatal heart attack on the way to pick me up!

They said they'd find someone else, and they did. When he arrived and we began driving to his home, he said, "We'll want to get you something to eat."

I certainly didn't expect anything fancy, but I asked him, "What is it you do?"

He said, "I'm in charge of catering for Swiss Air."

I ate very well on that trip. He had a wine cellar you would not believe.

It was a good trip all around. Jazz was really catching on in Europe. We played at a park in downtown Zurich and then at some village festivals. At one I had my first chance to play an alphorn. You'd likely recognize the instrument if you saw a picture—it's unwieldy, several meters long, a wooden horn that turns up at the end. The mouthpiece is cup shaped. It proved to be a little harder to play than I expected. I'll say this: I did make some sounds.

five

GIVING BACK

The year 1979 marked a decade for me at the University of Wisconsin. It was a natural time to take stock, which I did, though not in any formal way. I found myself thinking about what had transpired in the past ten years, and whether, looking to the future, I wanted to continue on the same path.

I felt good about what had been accomplished since I'd come to Madison. We'd rejuvenated the varsity band, which was now an integral part of both Badger basketball and Badger hockey games. The concert we'd begun in 1975 had, by 1979, become a rite of spring in Madison, and that April we sold out, with ninety-three hundred in the audience at the Field House.

As for the marching band, by 1979 it seemed like I was turning away more kids than I had been able to put on the field a decade earlier. We'd been getting plenty of favorable press, people saying it didn't matter so much anymore if the football team won at Camp Randall—fans were going to have a good time regardless because of the band. The Fifth Quarter started in 1978, the same year the good people of Providence gave the hockey fans and band a plaque for being the best in the country.

We'd also been strategic in our recruiting. We worked to get the message out that band was something any UW student could do. It was surprising how many were reluctant to try out because they thought they weren't good enough.

We set up a phone bank in the Humanities Building during registration week, and I asked the university to share the names of incoming students who'd had band in their junior or senior year in high school. I think we had four phone lines, and I had current band members make calls. They didn't hard sell it. But they'd say, "If you're interested in band, I can tell you I'm in the marching band right now and it's great." There was some pushback about the time it took, but my kids gave testimonials that it was time well spent.

The result was that, in 1979, I had around 325 kids try out for the band. I couldn't uniform that many and didn't want to. We started trying to tailor our recruiting to what we were going to need. What instruments were the senior class, soon to be graduating, playing? I had to think a year ahead just to ensure we would have enough tuba players, since they are highly visible. I recall one year having to try to find more trombones. Yet once the number trying out grew to over 300, it was clear we couldn't take everybody. I rejected one young man, Tim Kasino, three times. He came back as a senior and that year marched as an alternate. Mark Pynnonen played for eight years. He loved the band so much he would play in the fall, drop out of school for a semester, and return the following fall to both school and the band. The record for *consecutive* performances, however, belongs to Richard Tucker, a euphonium player. Starting in 1973, and continuing for seven years, Tucker marched in fifty consecutive pregame and half-time shows, never missing a performance.

The band's popularity, all the publicity—inevitably there were going to be some who saw it differently. By the mid-1980s, Ray Cramer, chair of the bands department at Indiana University, spoke to an Associated Press reporter who was doing a story on the UW Marching Band.

Cramer began by noting he was a friend and admirer of mine but added that he felt the Ohio State band best fit the image Big Ten bands were looking for.

"Ohio State stands in formation on the field and presents a very formal, straight, almost military type of show. They are very disciplined in their actions."

Cramer continued: "Then on the other side you have the Wisconsin band. The members break ranks to dance with the cheerleaders or pompom girls or maybe with each other, and let themselves show the good feelings that they're having. I don't think it's a matter of them intentionally creating a scene, but maybe it comes across to people at other schools as looking not very disciplined."

The story didn't bother me too much. I think Ray was right, at least from his perspective. The concept of the Fifth Quarter, for instance—some people just didn't get. I found I sometimes had to apologize for the band because they were just doing what we allowed them to do. We drew a line that said, "This is performance." But then there was the Fifth Quarter, and its charm was that we said, "OK, the formal part's over. Let your hair down." Some band directors I spoke with felt we were disrespectful. It was just what we did. We had to modify some things as we went along so people didn't think we were being disrespectful. But I can see it could come across that way.

Some band directors appreciated what we were doing. In that same Associated Press article, Craig Kirchhoff, director of bands at Ohio State (whose band Cramer had lauded), said this: "I think Mike is one of the most gifted people in the country, if not the most gifted, in dealing with marching bands. Mike is probably the master entertainer. And the band almost assumes Mike's personality."

Nice words, much appreciated. Of course, Craig had been a graduate assistant with me and the band in Madison!

As I reflected on a decade in Madison, I was proud of what we'd accomplished with the band. But that was also around the time that some people spoke with me about the possibility of going into administration. I did think about it, at least briefly. At one point I was nominated to be the assistant head of the UW School of Music. I didn't get it—there was an election and I didn't win. I felt bad at the time—as if it was a rebuke—but thank goodness I lost. I wouldn't have been happy in a desk job. Even at the time, I think I realized deep down that it wouldn't be wise for me to take a job with a lot of headaches and little joy. Why do that when I was having so much fun as things were?

Speaking of fun, the half-time show at the 1980 Homecoming football game against San Diego State was great fun. We brought back more than two hundred alumni members of the band to help with the festivities. We re-created the pregame run-on with them; some of the alumni had never participated in a run-on and were really up for it. Our band came out first, saluted Wisconsin and San Diego State, and then formed a tunnel at the north end zone for the alumni band to do the run-on. We then combined the bands for our Wisconsin version of the *1812 Overture*.

The bands joined forces at halftime, too, for "Varsity," with Ray Dvorak conducting. I'd often tried to include Ray. My first year, he conducted "Varsity" at every home game. After that he did it regularly, not every game, but maybe three or four times a year. He enjoyed it, and I was pleased to be able to facilitate that.

I mentioned earlier that one of my earliest drum majors, Ray Luick, came back for nearly all the alumni band festivities. While at UW, Ray became drum major for the Madison Scouts Drum and Bugle Corps.

Ray wasn't flashy as drum majors go, but he was steadfast. What I was looking for in a drum major—if I had to boil it down—was a leader: Someone the kids respected and did what he told them to do. Someone who could also see when things needed to be done. In a sense, another set of eyes for me on—and sometimes off—the field. My best drum majors had an ear for the social aspects of the band and could alert me if a faction was going rogue for one reason or another.

The on-field role of drum major in a marching band had evolved over time. In the old days it was a much more technical position. The drum major would give signals with his baton when the marchers were to change position. This had pretty well phased out by the time I was a band leader, though for a time we still made the drum majors learn the commands. But the routines were becoming more formalized, and the band members learned the moves on their own: sixteen steps one way, for instance, then thirty-two steps another, and so on.

As time went on, the drum major became more of a showman. In our band, this phenomenon was first personified in 1972 by John Strickler, who a year earlier had played cymbal in our percussion section. Before the decade of the 1970s was out, John's last name would become famous in UW athletic circles. Palmer "Butch" Strickler, John's father, was a butcher in New Glarus, near Madison, and a big booster of Badger sports. He was friendly with Elroy Hirsch and others in the department. In 1974, Strickler the elder threw his first "Butch's Baloney Bash" to benefit UW athletics. The event—which continued until 2002—grew in size and importance and raised hundreds of thousands of dollars. Often held in the Field House, the bash included abundant sausage and beer and a raffle that included some terrific prizes.

John Strickler and I agreed to try to change the image of the UW drum major, going from the staid British interpretation to a more freewheeling, or Americanized, style. John substituted a shorter, easier to twirl baton, arched his back while he marched, and wore riding breeches and boots. It was definitely showier.

I've had drum majors who were good at the show but none of the other things. I had another drum major who had talent but was clearly in it just for himself, which frustrated me. I finally said, "If you drop dead, don't do it on a yard line. We need the yard lines, but we don't need you."

Harsh, in hindsight, but we stressed team camaraderie during all my years with the band, and I had no time or need for prima donnas.

～

What a marching band always needs is a place to practice, and that became an issue for us in the early 1980s. Our practice facility on the west end of campus was usurped as part of an ambitious new building project for the first UW School of Veterinary Medicine. We subsequently shuttled among several different fields. All were in the general area of the Natatorium on Observatory Drive, but none were ideal. At first, Dave Berge, the director of Intramural Recreation at UW, found us a field but added a caveat: it's the athletic department's field; if they need it, you need to step aside. We had two other problems: there were no lights when it grew dark, as it does on late fall afternoons, and there was no place for instrument storage. We eventually raised money and had a brick building put up for the storage. For the lights, Berge worked out a deal that they'd light the soccer field, which was across the street, and we could use it when the sun went down. But we're hard on a field when we march, and we tore up the soccer field. Nobody was happy with us.

None of these fields drained well, and one year the kids were literally marching in ankle-deep mud. Why they stayed with me is a mystery. The *Wisconsin State Journal* illustrated the situation, on the front page of a 1982 Metro section, with two large photos of the band at practice: one at the start, when everyone is clean and dry, and a second below it from mid-practice, when everyone is caked with mud.

For a time, we even moved to Lot 60—a parking lot—to practice, but often cars were parked there, and even when there were no cars, there was the risk of marching into cement light poles.

We finally ended up on a field on Marsh Lane just north and east of the Wisconsin Alumni Research Foundation tower. Berge told me, "If you can raise the money for an artificial turf field, we'll make it the permanent practice home of the marching band."

That's what happened. It helped with the sloppy conditions, but it didn't alleviate all our issues. The marching takes a toll even on the artificial turf, and we had to replace it a couple of times. We still had no lights. At first the athletic department let us practice in Camp Randall when it grew dark late in the season. If the team was using the stadium field, we'd go inside to what is now known as the McClain Center.

What happened, of course, is that the athletic department folks began seeing wear and depression on the fields. They weren't wrong. There is a lot of intensity when a marching band musician puts his or her foot down. My system of charting routines had the musicians moving four steps off the yard line each way. If they were doing it right, those four steps were hitting the same reference point each time, not good for wear and tear.

At one point it was suggested that I change our marching style. I said that wasn't going to happen. In the end, they supplied the band members with football shoes, thinking that the synthetic turf might come with the cleats during a step, negating any depression. It did help, and the kids felt as if they'd been given something by athletics, which they appreciated. I liked the uniformity it produced.

~

It was at a band practice one day circa 1980 when I first noticed a young man who would become an honorary member of the marching band. Steve Singel just showed up at the practice field one afternoon. I learned later that he lived nearby with his parents.

Steve was born with Down syndrome. His father and mother, Ray and Elaine Singel, were to my mind exemplary parents for a family dealing with a developmental disability. When Steve was born in Beaver Dam in 1952, the Singels were told that he would likely never walk or

I'm pictured here with Steve Singel, who began as a spectator and became an important part of our band family. (Gary Smith)

talk. They didn't believe that and rightly so: Steve did both. Ray and Elaine encouraged Steve but didn't coddle him. Consequently he was independent, and an achiever. Steve participated in Special Olympics, was employed at the Madison Opportunity Center, and was honored by the Rotary Club of South Madison with its Service Above Self award. A newspaper story at the time noted that Steve "directs the UW–Madison pep band when it plays 'If You Want to Be a Badger' at basketball games and brings up the rear when the tuba section of the marching band weaves its way around Camp Randall at football games."

Steve did more than that for us. He was in his twenties when he first showed up at band practice. He'd clap his hands and march near the tubas. He was a talker, and soon was asking me questions about the band. I gave him little tasks to do, which he enjoyed. He came to practice so often I said only half-jokingly he was at more rehearsals than some of the clarinet players.

The kids in the band really took to him. Eventually we initiated an award in Steve's name that the band voted on. It went to the band member who was not necessarily the most gifted musician but who best exemplified Steve's attitude and spirit. Steve would come to the year-end banquet, and I'd ask him to present the award plaque. He did, but not before taking the microphone and saying a few words, or more than a few words, which everyone loved.

In 1985, Very Special Arts Wisconsin was accredited by the national organization, and a state office was established in Madison. Its charter, as I noted earlier when describing our first appearance at Lambeau, was to provide arts programming for people with disabilities. They'd noticed that Steve Singel had adopted the UW Marching Band and the band had adopted Steve. VSA Wisconsin reached out and asked if I would like to be on its board.

I felt if I was going to be on the board, I wanted to do something to support the organization. In 1988, we started the VSA/UW Marching Band Program. It paired high school students with disabilities with members of their respective high school bands. The band members tutored the VSA students on music and marching, and on one Saturday each football season, we invited all the participating students—two hundred from around Wisconsin—to come to Camp Randall and play with the UW Marching Band as the Very Special Arts Marching Band. The music was not especially remarkable, but the kids had a ball, and each year the scene was joyful.

My association with VSA Wisconsin continued, and in 1998 I co-chaired, with Wisconsin First Lady Sue Ann Thompson, the Capitol Open Golf Tournament, which raised $47,000 for VSA Wisconsin (including a matching grant from AT&T). The organization, which continues to thrive, is now known as ARTS for ALL Wisconsin.

~

We were always willing to try new things with the band, and as you might guess, some worked and endured while others did not. For a few years, starting in 1979, the band played a Field House show on the Friday night before the Homecoming football game. We were asked to do it after the big-name entertainment brought in for the show became prohibitively expensive. We played with the Wisconsin Singers the first couple of years, then took a year off, and in 1982 served as the Homecoming Eve opening act for Gallagher, "The World's Craziest Comic."

We drew only fifteen hundred people for the 1982 show, but the *Wisconsin State Journal* review was rapturous, noting that "the band and their reverberations put the audience in a wild and festive mood that was retained throughout the evening."

Speaking of the Field House acoustics, Gallagher said, "The band will come out and play for half an hour and then their echo will play for half an hour."

Around this time, I also conducted an annual show with the UW Concert Band, which consisted of good players who were not quite the equal of the Wind Ensemble, the number-one concert group. The Concert Band was a talented junior varsity, if you will. We tried to do concerts that would get people's attention, often with a family-oriented theme.

In 1981, we played an all–John Philip Sousa concert and tried to replicate all facets of a Sousa concert. We dressed like Sousa. I wore a 1915 band uniform—without question 100 percent wool. After every major selection, we played a march, because that's what Sousa did. Ray Dvorak was the one who told me that: if you played the *William Tell Overture*, the next piece would be a march, and so on. It turned out that UW's music library had a lot of tunes Sousa had performed. I tried to make the concert as authentic as I could.

We must have done OK, because the following year people were asking for more Sousa. I decided to stick with a band heritage theme, but instead put together a show of circus music, which is one of the oldest kinds of band music. We held the concert in the Stock Pavilion and dressed the band in red coats and bow ties, in the manner of the old Ringling Brothers bands. I shared a phone call with Merle Evans, who spent three decades as bandmaster for the Ringling Brothers circus. People who know circus music know that it is demanding from an endurance and technical standpoint. Circus bands often had some of the finest musicians around, given the shorter symphony seasons in earlier eras. We didn't aim that high, but we had fun. Our big challenge was pacing the music with the jugglers and clowns who were also part of the show.

The year of our Sousa show, 1981, also marked the return of the UW football team to a bowl game for the first time since the 1963 Rose Bowl and only the fourth bowl appearance ever. The Badgers were playing the University of Tennessee in the Garden State Bowl that December. It was a big enough deal that Elroy Hirsch called me into his office and said he wanted the entire marching band to make the trip east—the game was to be played at Giants Stadium in New Jersey. More than that, the athletic department would pay for it. In the end we took 220 kids—a dozen or so stayed back in Madison for academic reasons. It was a great trip. I think half the kids in the band had never been on an airplane before. They stayed four to a room in the Saddle Brook, New Jersey, Marriott and had a ball. The day before the game they toured Manhattan. Earlier that morning, at a practice at Giants Stadium, we acquired a big psychological edge on the Tennessee band, which was also at the stadium. It was cold with a dusting of snow on the field, and their people were in heavy coats and scarves. Ours came out in sweat-shirts and shorts. No question who was tougher!

We played before and after the game and at halftime, when our theme was "Badgers on Broadway." We played the tune "On Broad-way" and numerous songs from *West Side Story*. The Badgers lost the game, 28–21, but in the unbiased opinion of all our fans, won the half-time going away.

~

The following fall, 1982, the Badgers played three football games that are worth remembering. The band was there for all three.

The first game was in October in Columbus, Ohio, where the Badgers had not won a football game against Ohio State since 1918—sixty-four years! It was a rainy day and when Wisconsin went ahead 6–0 early, missing the extra point after a touchdown, I had a photographer shoot a photo of me in front of the scoreboard. I said to one of my assistants, "I like seeing Wisconsin ahead. I'm afraid it won't last." Somehow, how-ever, that score held up all game long and the Badgers prevailed 6–0. UW head coach Dave McClain called it the biggest win of his career, bigger even than when he took his Ball State team back to his alma mater, Bowling Green, and emerged victorious. McClain had coached at Ohio State under Woody Hayes, so winning in Columbus was huge. McClain had brought the Badgers for the first time three years earlier and been bludgeoned, 59–0.

I took a "mini band" into the jubilant Wisconsin locker room after the game: three trombones, three trumpets, and a tuba. It was enough to play a stirring rendition of "You've Said It All."

Just two weeks later, there was a game at Camp Randall that has a storied place in Badger lore. It's known as the "bounce pass game," but you'll forgive me for thinking that it was the game when the band's Fifth Quarter became truly legendary.

Illinois was the visiting team. With just over a minute to go in the game, the Badgers were trailing the Illini, 26–22. Wisconsin had the ball on the Illinois forty-yard line. Quarterback Randy Wright took the snap and immediately threw a pass sideways to the great Badger wide receiver Al Toon. The pass was underthrown, bounced on the turf, and into Toon's hands.

It was a trick play.

Toon had taken two or three steps backward, so Wright's pass was in fact a lateral, and the ball's hitting the turf did not stop play. Wright bounced it on purpose. Now Toon looked downfield, and as the Badgers had hoped, another receiver, Jeff Nault, was wide open. The Illini defenders had stopped, thinking Wright had thrown an incomplete pass.

Toon threw the ball downfield to Nault, who caught it and trotted into the end zone, a forty-yard touchdown pass. The Badgers now led 28–26. There were fifty-two seconds left.

Which, unfortunately, proved to be enough time for Illinois to mount a last-second comeback and kick a forty-six-yard field goal to beat the Badgers, 29–28. UW had snatched defeat from the jaws of victory in stunning fashion. Still, it had been a terrific game with an amazing finish, and I thought—rightly as it turned out—that the crowd likely still had some pent-up energy. I told the band this was our moment.

"Mike Leckrone's band assembled on the field for their usual postgame show," *State Journal* sports editor Glenn Miller noted the next day. "You would not think this would be one of the biggest shows in history [but] if you thought that, you would be wrong. This was the biggest show of all. What were all those fans doing, standing at their seats, cheering like Wisconsin had just won a big victory? It is truly hard to understand, but that was what was happening."

Miller was not the only observer wide-eyed at what was taking place. The sports editor was standing next to Big Ten commissioner Wayne Duke, who turned to Miller and said, "It could not happen anywhere else."

That December, the football Badgers played in their second consecutive bowl game, the Independence Bowl in Shreveport, Louisiana, against Kansas State. The band again was able to go. But the rain in Shreveport made what happened earlier at Ohio State seem like a passing shower. It rained every day we were in Louisiana. I recall having to

Before I learned to fly at the UW Varsity Band concerts, the New Glarus fire department helped me to new heights at Camp Randall. (Gary Smith)

cancel a band practice, and I don't cancel practice lightly. Elroy Hirsch was desperate for us to have a pregame pep rally. I told him it was going to be pouring and there was no place for it. But Elroy found a cow barn, not far from the stadium. "We can fix it up and you can have it there," Elroy said. It smelled like a cow barn—there was no mistaking it for anything else—but again the fans showed up, and this time, once we made it to Independence Stadium and the game, the team did, too, in a big way. The Badgers beat the Wildcats, 14–3. It was UW's first-ever victory in a bowl game. I remember being soaking wet and not caring. It was a great feeling. Coincidentally, that Independence Bowl was the first college football game televised live by a fledgling sports network called ESPN.

~

The following spring the band and I participated in a wonderfully wacky Madison tradition, a boom box parade around the Capitol Square and down State Street. The parade on June 1, 1983, was the third one organized by Leon Varjian, a former Wisconsin Student Association vice president and the mind responsible for such famed Madison pranks as the "sunken" Statue of Liberty on Lake Mendota and the thousand plastic pink flamingoes planted on Bascom Hill.

I really didn't know Leon well, but I liked him. I seem to gravitate to people who are by conventional standards a bubble or two off plumb. I wonder why that is?

Instead of instruments that day, the band carried boom boxes, which played Sousa marches, courtesy of Sauk City radio station WSEY. Leon's unit was clad in old uniforms of the Indiana University Marching 100, which he had purchased at auction while studying for a master's degree in Bloomington.

In September 1983, a recording by our marching band, *Echoes from Camp Randall*, became the first album released by the UW School of Music on its new record label. We'd recorded it the previous March during a long afternoon in the UW Stock Pavilion with WHA Radio recording engineer Marv Nonn. It was long in part because of interruptions by a thunderstorm and two trains passing nearby. We played songs people expected—"On, Wisconsin!," "If You Want to Be a Badger," "You've Said It All"—but some maybe they wouldn't expect, including James Taylor's "Country Road" and Marvin Hamlisch's "Nobody Does It Better." When Gary Peterson reviewed the album—highly favorably—in the *Capital Times*, he listed our *1812 Overture* and "Space Badgers" as particular favorites.

The album did well. A company in Arizona handled the pressing of five thousand discs, and UW music students sold them for seven dollars outside Camp Randall at home football games.

~

In spring 1984, I was presented with one of the more unusual and, as it turned out, memorable opportunities of my career. I took a call from Bill Moffit, who was then the director of the Purdue University "All-American" Marching Band, and a good friend of mine. We knew each other from having worked at numerous clinics and guest-conducting gigs together. Bill was a colorful character and an innovator in marching band style and music. I believe more than a thousand—some huge number—of his marching band arrangements were published, and he helped me get a few published too.

In the phone call Bill said he'd been asked about conducting a show in late June at the Hollywood Bowl in Los Angeles. He either couldn't do it or didn't want to and asked if he could put the organizers in touch with me. I said certainly. Who wouldn't want to conduct in the Hollywood Bowl? Bill noted that I'd be conducting the Gay Bands of America. I doubt Bill thought I'd have any problem with that, but I assured him immediately that I didn't.

It turned out the event was an AIDS benefit, timed for late June and the fifteenth anniversary of the Stonewall riots in New York City in 1969, when police raided a popular gay bar on Christopher Street in Greenwich Village.

"A Gay Night at the Bowl" was sponsored by a group called Christo-pher Street West. They wanted me to conduct what was essentially an all-star band of gay and lesbian musicians from across the country— terrific professional players from symphonies in Dallas, Philadelphia, and other major cities. They also wanted me to conduct a part of the evening's stage show, which would feature Rita Moreno.

I was all in, but I went to speak with Eunice Meske (later Eunice Boardman), who was chair of the UW School of Music, to tell her about the invitation. She encouraged me.

"I don't know how you can not do it," Eunice said.

One thing to remember is that 1984 was a different time in terms of wide public acceptance of gays and lesbians. The scourge of AIDS was beginning to take its terrible toll on gay men.

Many years later I saw an interview with Rita Moreno in which she recalled doing the "Gay Night at the Bowl" and echoed what Eunice had said to me in 1984.

"We did a Hollywood Bowl fundraiser—and what a show," Moreno said. "My daughter Fernanda, who was sixteen at the time, danced with me. To show you how early this was, the press showed up and exclaimed, 'Why are you doing this?' The implication being that this could be bad publicity. I answered, 'Why wouldn't I?'"

I remember Rita dancing with her daughter that night. I also remem-ber feeling privileged to be able to conduct these world-class musicians in such an iconic venue. Phyllis accompanied me to California, and the whole week was remarkable. A limousine drove us around. They took Phyllis shopping while I was rehearsing. Two days after the concert, we served as marshals at a Gay Pride Parade in Los Angeles. That was quite a production too. I recall looking up the street from our booth and see-ing a group of motorcycles approaching, the riders dressed as cowboys. Or so I thought. I could tell they were all wearing chaps. When they passed us, I could see they were wearing chaps and, well, nothing else.

Once they found out I was straight—it took a while—the musicians had a lot of good-natured humor at my expense, which I attempted to return in kind. The double entendres were flying. All told, looking back on the experience, I don't think I ever had a better time as a guest conductor.

~

Around the same time as the Hollywood Bowl invitation, I was one of sixteen American composers asked to write a trumpet fanfare for the 1984 Summer Olympic Games in Los Angeles. Again my friend Bill Moffit was involved, informing the Olympics organizers that I'd written numerous arrangements for marching bands and suggesting they reach out to me.

It was an honor to be asked, and I contributed a short—twenty seconds—fanfare that would be played by Aida trumpets, instruments designed to play the "Grand March" of Verdi's opera. We were told not to make the pieces too difficult. I didn't hear it live on the Olympics telecast, but I did hear a recording of it later. Part of what made the Olympics invitation a kick was that two of my marching band members, Bill Walker and Jay Beckman, were selected to play in the Olympics band. Bill played trumpet, and Jay played a euphonium, which looks a bit like a baby tuba—a tuba with less tubing. It's sometimes called the cello of the brass section, and produces a gorgeous, mellow sound.

I'd been writing—and publishing—music for a long time when I received the Olympics invitation. During my time at Butler, Jim Houston, a friend and fellow musician and music educator, started a music publishing company in Lebanon, Indiana, called Studio P/R. Jim asked if I could write a couple of pieces for his fledgling company, and I said I would.

I regard writing music, which I've continued to do throughout my life, as the more serious side of my career. Frankly, I think there were people in the UW School of Music who weren't sure I could read music, let alone write it. To those people I was an entertainer, and certainly that is a big part of who I am. But when I started, I never thought I'd be a marching band director, so concert band, and writing concert pieces, was something I embraced early and continued.

It's hard, writing music. You start with a blank sheet of paper and hope for an idea. I had an instructor who said the first thing you have to do is get the paper dirty—start marking the measures, so that physically you're doing something. Sometimes it's musical, sometimes you have a phrase. Something that gets you started and you expand on. Often it's a melodic line, or an image. A good example came about a year and a half after I had heart surgery. I was commissioned to write a piece. I wrote one I called "Arrhythmia," and I filled it with different tempos and meters to conjure an ongoing sense of uneasiness.

I usually do three or four drafts of every piece. Once I have an idea of the melody, I'll see how I can harmonize it and make it rhythmically unique. I had an arranging teacher once who counseled us to find a way so that everyone who will be playing will like the piece. You can do that by giving every player something special—even if it's very small and consists of playing easy whole notes for the balance of the piece.

As I said, it's hard, and can be mentally draining. It's very difficult to write something that is both playable and unique. I could write music that is truly unique, but nobody could play it. And to me the whole idea of writing music is to get people to play it.

Back when I was writing for Jim Houston and Studio P/R, he asked me to write a piece that could be played by a symphonic band.

"A symphonic march," Jim said. "We'll figure out a title later."

I wrote the piece, and Jim acquired the rights to use the title "Tower of the Americas," which, of course, is the name of the 750-foot tower that was constructed in the 1960s in San Antonio. When we released the piece, I wrote an explanatory sidebar in which I said the grandeur of the architecture had moved me to write the music as I did. Shameless! I'd never seen it when I wrote the piece.

The best moment of writing any piece comes when you actually hear it played live. With a synthesizer you can get an idea of what you're going to hear, but it's not the same.

I've written quite a few pieces I'm proud of, including one from 1983 called "Intrusions." Another that sold well was 1974's "Avatara." I'll mention one more: a piece called "Episodions," for which I took inspiration from an ancient musical composition called "Seikilos Epitaph," using its melody as the basis for a new piece that I then christened with a Greek-inspired name.

~

At some point in the early 1980s, it dawned on us that 1985 would mark the one-hundredth anniversary of the UW Marching Band. We decided to celebrate the centennial with a special half-time performance in 1985 and then an extra-special outdoor show at Camp Randall Stadium the following spring.

In the meantime, I'd begun gathering material for a book that would salute the band's history. *Songs to Thee Wisconsin: 100 Years, the University of Wisconsin Bands* was published in spring 1985. It was hardcover, 240 pages, and contained everything from the origins of some of our most iconic songs to a complete roster of the men and women who had played in the band over the past century. That section filled thirty pages and contained eight thousand names!

I spent much of summer 1984 doing the research for the book. The idea came from some other marching bands with distinguished histories. Nebraska and Ohio State had done centennial books, and I ordered those to see how they went about it. I consulted books on the history of UW–Madison and spent considerable time in the university archive. Ray Dvorak had kept a scrapbook, somewhat spotty and incomplete but useful, nonetheless.

I uncovered numerous fascinating accounts of the band's early years, foremost its 1915 trip by railroad to a world's fair in San Francisco. The fair's proper name was the Panama-Pacific International Exposition. The State of Wisconsin had an exhibit at the fair, and UW School of Music head Jesse Saugstad and band director Charles Mann thought it should be supplemented with some Wisconsin music. They approached various entities for funding for the band's trip, including the Legislature. Approval was not forthcoming. At nearly the last minute, the UW Board of Regents stepped up and guaranteed funding.

What a trip it proved to be. San Francisco was the destination, but the UW band—referred to as the First Regiment Band, a nod to its military roots—played its way to California. In all the band traveled more than seven thousand miles through fourteen states, during which it performed more than one hundred times.

After the band's June 1915 concert in Great Falls, Montana, the *Great Falls Tribune* published a rapturous review that read in part:

> They gave to their audience one of the best musical programs ever rendered here by a band and one that, measured purely on the thrills of delight which it produced, probably has not been equaled. Other bands may have provided as good music, possibly better, but who can deny there is a charm about the appearance of a lot of clean, bright, interesting college boys that cannot be found in the professional musician. So it was with the program last night . . .
>
> It was evident to all who heard the band that the state of Wisconsin is well represented abroad when its university band is on tour, and the people who are fortunate enough to live in the course of its path to the world's fair town of San Francisco, or those who happen to cross its path at the fair, will have plenty of pleasure for an evening and a very happy memory.

I chuckled when I read the following at the close of the review: "After the concert, several members of the band went to the palm room of Hotel Rainbow, where they further popularized themselves by playing until midnight."

Some things didn't change across the ensuing century!

That 1915 band had the kind of camaraderie that I believe is perhaps the most enduring legacy of the marching band experience at Wisconsin. What do students remember five, ten, or twenty years after graduating? I would argue it's not classrooms. The band members remember the friendships that come from performing, socializing, and—yes—sometimes suffering together. A bond develops that is not divisible.

Members of the 1915 band that went to San Francisco gathered annually in Madison on Homecoming eve for the next fifty-plus years. In November 1966 the Homecoming reunion was a dinner at Ray Dvorak's home on Jefferson Street. They read letters from absent members and paid tribute to members who had died.

Two decades later, I introduced Frank Fosgate, one of the 1915 band members who was present at Ray's house that night, at an alumni band banquet on Friday, October 11, 1985, at the Field House to celebrate the band's centennial.

All told, some seven hundred band alumni were on hand for our centennial weekend celebration, which included special pregame, half-time, and postgame performances before the Iowa game at Camp Randall on October 12. I specifically chose a game three weeks in advance of Homecoming to give the centennial its own special due.

The Friday night banquet at the Field House drew 450 people, a mix of band alumni, dignitaries, and fans. Remarks were made by Chancellor Irv Shain, Bob Rennebohm of the UW Foundation, music school director Eunice Meske, and me. Everyone in attendance received a black-and-white print of Old Music Hall and the Humanities Building, courtesy of the Dvorak family as a tribute to Ray, who died in 1982. Ray's son, Robert, did the artwork.

Attendees also received miniature replicas of the Paul Bunyan drum—a huge drum that was presented to the UW Marching Band in 1935 by an Elks Lodge in Appleton upon the band's fiftieth anniversary. It pictured Paul Bunyan on the side, axe on his shoulder, and noted "University of Wisconsin Bands" at the top and "Founded 1885" at the bottom.

Alas, the drum never made the trip from Old Music Hall to the Humanities Building, so we made a replica for our half-time show the day after the banquet. Other salutes to the past during that show included showcasing a 1920s sousaphone in which the bell faced up—hence its nickname, "the rain catcher."

The pregame run-on included 470 band alumni, all wearing red, in waves that seemed might never end. By the time they did, an entire half of the field was filled, fifty-yard line to the back of the end zone and all the way across. At halftime, the number of band alumni on the field swelled to 720. It was an amazing day.

Nearly lost in the embrace of the past was the fact that halftime also brought the introduction of a matched set of trumpets and trombones, which marked an upgrade in sound quality unmatched in the sixteen years I'd been in Madison. It also looked far superior to the ragtag mix of silver and brass, big and little instruments we'd had in the past. Players would come to rehearsals with junk instruments. I couldn't blame them. If you take a Bach trumpet out on the field and someone runs into you, your $1,000 horn is damaged. Players would show up with tarnished instruments, whatever they had, and it just looked ugly. I kept harping on it and eventually we found solutions.

The 1985 trombones and trumpets were courtesy of UW graduate Carleton Holstrom, an Appleton native and investment banking executive, and Don Getzen, from D.E.G. Music Products Company. The centennial trumpets and trombones had a special silver finish and a one-hundredth-anniversary logo engraved in the bell.

In 1990, Holstrom initiated another significant gift to the band, which included euphoniums, flugelhorns, clarinets, and saxophones—along with tubas and percussion for the varsity band. The association with Getzen continued as well. In 2002, the company owner and president, Tom Getzen, remarked, "We are proud to continue to be part of the Badger Band's trademark sound. The Badger Band has been using Getzen silver plated trumpets, trombones, and flugelhorns for several years and it is always a thrill to hear our instruments being played by a band of this caliber."

∼

I was always careful to work with the university administration and make sure things were done appropriately when corporate affiliations were proposed. Back in the early 1980s, Anheuser-Busch contacted the athletic department looking for some sort of mutually beneficial arrangement centered on the band's enormously popular "You've Said It All"—our version of the "Bud" theme song.

They wound up producing two television commercials with the band playing and our fans screaming, "When you say WIS-CON-SIN, you've said it all." The spots were in good taste, nothing tacky—basically Anheuser-Busch tipping its hat to our band, the university, and the state of Wisconsin. There was no formal contract, but the brewery made several donations: to the band's travel budget, the athletic department for scholarships, and to WHA-TV to help underwrite delayed telecasts of Badger football games.

No surprise, I suppose, that the commercials were controversial in some quarters. The NCAA looked into whether any athletes or band members were paid to appear (they weren't).

The *Wisconsin State Journal* put the appropriateness of the commercials as one of two questions in its January 1982 readers' poll. The other question involved whether President Reagan was right to place sanctions on the Soviet Union over its martial law policy in Poland.

I was interested to see that nearly twice as many people voted on the Budweiser commercial question as on the Reagan sanctions.

I was heartened, too, that the response was overwhelmingly positive toward the Bud-band TV spots, with 217 readers in favor and 47 opposed.

A woman from McFarland wrote: "As a mother of a member of the marching band, I feel that being chosen for this commercial was an honor bestowed on an outstanding group of young people who have given many long, hard hours of practice to achieve this recognition."

And another woman, writing from Madison: "Budweiser benefits, UW benefits. Why not? We adopted their song and they're saying thanks. Why take a fun idea so seriously?"

The topic occasionally resurfaced. At the end of our 1985 centennial year, UW–Madison dean of students Paul Ginsberg suggested publicly that retiring "You've Said It All" might be a necessary component of discouraging excessive alcohol consumption on campus.

Few seemed to agree, and at least one man in a position of influence pushed back strongly. Wisconsin state Senator Carl Otte drafted a letter to Ginsberg saying the dean had analyzed the situation in precisely the wrong way.

"The 'Bud Song' has brought national acclaim to the University," Otte, whose letter found its way into the press, wrote. "It has become a symbol of the enthusiasm and support the fans of this state have for the UW athletic teams and the band . . . If you were truly concerned about the image of the University of Wisconsin you would be doing everything possible to promote, rather than ban, the 'Bud Song.'"

I might note that earlier that year, the state Senate gave me and the band a special citation honoring our centennial. We performed that day in the capitol rotunda, and, yes, we played "You've Said It All."

What UW Marching Band alumnus joined us, playing the tuba he still kept in his office? State Senator Carl Otte, of course.

～

The year 1985 ended and the controversy involving Dean Ginsberg faded away—but our centennial celebration didn't. Looking toward May 1986, we'd planned a stand-alone centennial concert at Camp Randall Stadium. It proved quite an extravaganza, certainly the biggest UW band concert ever, in front of perhaps the biggest musical audience to that time in Madison. An estimated seventeen thousand people paid five dollars a ticket to see the show, and I'm confident they got their money's worth and more. In the days leading up to the May 9 performance, I worried much more about the possibility of bad weather than bad music. We were ready, and the weather cooperated.

We had a forty-by-eighty-foot roof-covered stage flanked by thirty-five-foot-high acoustical wings and two large closed-circuit television screens. There were fireworks and a laser show for which I needed FAA clearance—planes flying overhead had to be warned about the lasers.

The show was in three parts: a parade of musical groups to present a history of wind music; the marching band, of course; and finally a stage show. The parade included the First Brigade Band of Milwaukee, a sixty-member troupe that specialized in Civil War music, utilizing that era's instruments as well. Other performers included Madison Area Technical College's Jazz Ensemble; Doc DeHaven's Dixieland band; and Doc's daughter Kelly DeHaven, a terrific vocalist.

I was gratified to read a report on the show a few days later in the *Capital Times*, not a review in the entertainment pages but rather an appreciation on the editorial page:

It was the Fifth Quarter magnified a dozen times. The band, of course, was the highlight of the evening, bringing the crowd to its feet for a stomping good time. But the whole evening was a musical extravaganza that no doubt left the 17,000 fans who gathered in the stands feeling as revved up as the fireworks crackling over the stadium and the light show flashing in front of them.

Thanks to the band and to director Mike Leckrone for a splendid show! For 100 years, the UW Marching Band has been part of the magic of the university and seldom has that magic been as tangible as it was Friday night. This is an event worth repeating in future years.

It was a wonderful way to begin the band's second century.

six

FOOTBALL FIZZLES BUT THE BAND PLAYS ON

On a Monday afternoon less than two weeks before our outdoor centennial show at Camp Randall, UW's head football coach, Dave McClain,
rode an exercise bike in the team's training room, then walked into the
sauna. Minutes later, someone entered the sauna to retrieve a towel. He
spoke to McClain, who was lying on an upper bench, but the coach
didn't respond. He'd suffered a fatal heart attack, at age forty-eight.

It shocked me, as it did all of Madison and beyond, though Dave had
a family history of heart disease. Of all the Badger coaches I've known
over the years, Dave and his wife, Judy, were among those Phyllis and I
were closest to. We were at their home numerous times. Dave was a little
on the gruff side, not touchy-feely, but I liked that. He was a good friend.

One of McClain's assistants, Jim Hilles, was named interim head
coach for the 1986 season. It was a tough assignment by any measure,
and the team, unfortunately, did not have a good year on the field,
compiling a 3–9 record.

For the band, there was excitement over a scheduled trip to Las Vegas
in mid-September 1986, when the Badger football team would be playing the University of Nevada, Las Vegas (UNLV). It was a three-day trip
that included 240 members of the marching band—and an estimated
fifteen thousand Badger fans who couldn't resist the lure of a rollicking
time in Vegas.

We did our part to enhance the fun, but first we had a rehearsal on the UNLV practice field. It was hot, and after an hour and a half of rehearsal, nobody much minded when the field's sprinkler system went on without warning.

It had been arranged for us to play a pep rally for the Badger faithful the day before the game. With remarkable cooperation from city officials, two blocks of Fremont Street in downtown Las Vegas were cordoned off, and we performed for an overflowing, boisterous crowd of red-attired fans. The day of the game we rehearsed in the parking lot of the MGM Hotel. Word got around Vegas—this visiting band rocked! Our half-time show at the stadium drew a standing ovation. All told, the trip was good preparation for some even more ambitious adventures that were still a few years away.

At the end of the 1986 football season, interim head coach Hilles was not retained. The university hired forty-year-old Don Morton, who had won an NCAA Division II title at North Dakota State and coached two years at the University of Tulsa before joining the Badgers. Shortly after Morton was hired, Ade Sponberg, his athletic director at North Dakota State, was tapped to replace the retiring Elroy Hirsch as UW athletic director. For both men the Big Ten conference proved a difficult step up from Division II.

Let me say that I liked both Don and Ade personally. Nice guys, supportive of the band. But there is no denying that when the football team began to rack up losses, beginning in 1987 and continuing across three seasons, it changed the dynamic at Camp Randall Stadium, which meant things changed for the band too. Morton's teams were 6–27 in 1987–89, and just 3–21 in Big Ten conference games.

There was a feeling—I felt it, and I think the band did too—that we had to try to pick up the slack and do our best to retain a festive atmosphere at Camp Randall. *Pressure* is not the right word for what we felt. It was more like: nothing else is going right, let's see what we can come up with that will be entertaining, and keep things fun.

Being honest, I think we were allowed to do some things in those years that at another time would have been considered not appropriate, or dangerous, or taking away from the game. In the Morton era there just wasn't much game from which to detract. I met numerous times with Bob Leu, who served several marketing functions in the athletic department, to discuss ways the band could help during this bleak time.

For one thing, we began to send traveling bands around the stadium. Smaller groups, maybe ten to fifteen musicians, would walk around and engage with fans, playing "On, Wisconsin!" or another of our standards. We had some general rules: It could begin only after halftime. Play only when the game on the field is stopped, not during the action. It started with the musicians doing it on their own, but fairly quickly I realized I needed to have them clear it with me, because I still needed a band seated to play during the third-quarter break, and after touchdowns. A couple of times I looked around and there weren't many left seated in the band.

Several things eventually became staples of the Fifth Quarter. There was the chicken dance, an idea that longtime Badger crew coach Randy "Jabo" Jablonic, a friend of the band, offered after visiting a beer hall in Germany. Then Matt Whiting, one of the leaders of the band who could spontaneously get a lot of things going, began doing the "tequila dance." It had been popularized a year or two earlier by Pee-wee Herman in his movie *Pee-wee's Big Adventure*.

Matt later became a field assistant for me. He was a graduate of McFarland High School and was taught there by a man named Bill Garvey, who was in my first band at UW. Bill started as a trumpet player but the tuba players took hold of him, and he switched to tuba. Bill, like Matt after him, became a field assistant upon graduating. He stayed decades—Bill was among the most passionate Badgers I ever met. Eventually Bill's daughter, Jessica, would be a member of our marching band.

Bill Garvey taught at McFarland High School for thirty-one years. When he died at age sixty, far too soon, of cancer in May 2012, there was an extraordinary two-day tribute in McFarland, first at the school, then at Lewis Park. The UW Marching Band played. The actor and Broadway star Tom Wopat, a friend of the band and Garvey's college roommate, came from New York to honor his friend. Thousands of others paid respects.

Matt Whiting provided a wonderful tribute to Bill in an interview he gave *Madison Magazine* at the time.

"He found a way to find the diamond in the rough of everyone," Matt said, "and work with it to help them develop. That's what he did with me. He changed my life. He changed a lot of lives."

~

One incident seems to symbolize the 1987–89 era at Camp Randall Stadium—a time of bad breaks and cascading losses. It happened during our half-time show when the Badgers hosted the University of Illinois Fighting Illini on October 15, 1988.

We had planned an ambitious, circus-themed half-time show. I'd become friendly with the Zor Shrine Circus folks through our mutual participation in the annual UW Homecoming Parade. We were usually lined up near each other, and I would joke about not wanting to be too close behind the camels.

That friendship resulted in our calling on them occasionally for help with our shows, and they were always obliging. One time we had a country and western–themed performance, and I ended the show riding a palomino horse up the tunnel, while the band played "Happy Trails," the Roy Rogers theme song. The Zor folks gave me a red cowboy hat that I waved to the crowd as I rode out.

My friendship with the Zor Shriners and the fact that Circus World Museum is in nearby Baraboo made a circus-themed Camp Randall show seem like a natural. We made plans for clowns, acrobats, a calliope in the south end zone, and three-ring, simultaneous performances.

At one point during the preparation I said, offhandedly, "Let's get an elephant. You can't have a circus without an elephant."

People were a bit leery. I said, "Circus World Museum will help us find an elephant."

They did—her name was Molly. Funny what you never forget. Of course, once we had Molly, we had to figure out what to do with her. We didn't want her out on the field too long, and we certainly didn't want her just wandering around. We decided that the thing to do would be to have her make a dramatic entrance, and she did.

Here's what happened that afternoon: My assistant took over the conducting of one of the tunes, and I ran up the tunnel, where Molly and her trainer were waiting for me. I put on a circus-style jacket, climbed aboard, and Molly and I came lumbering back down the tunnel, with her trainer trotting alongside.

The trainer had told me: "We don't think she's going to get spooked. She's around people all the time at Circus World." Then he added, "But she's an animal. You never know."

Well, Molly began by doing exactly what she was supposed to do. We got to the fifty-yard line, directly in front of the Badgers' bench. There she was supposed to kneel. I'd get off and take over conducting the band again.

But while Molly was still standing, I heard the crowd roar.

I remember thinking, "We really struck a nerve! They love it!"

What had happened was that Molly had deposited an elephant-sized dump on the fifty-yard line.

The trainer was embarrassed. Earlier I'd asked him: "Is there any danger of her crapping on the field?"

"We'll empty her out right before we take her on the field," he said.

They miscalculated empty.

I did think it was funny in retrospect. At the time, the field crew had to try to clean it up in a hurry, and the only pressurized water available was in a far corner of the field. A hose had to be located. The water finally started shooting out, and in combination with some shoveling the field was cleared.

Not that it helped Wisconsin. The referees assessed the Badgers a five-yard delay-of-game penalty, and in the end the Illini trounced them, 34–6. *Wisconsin State Journal* sportswriter Vic Feuerherd noted in the next day's paper: "The stench emanating from Camp Randall in the second half had nothing to do with an elephant's deposit at midfield . . . It was the smell of the Badgers getting burned for 27 points during an eight-and-a-half-minute stretch of the third and fourth quarters."

∼

The collapse of the football program had a ripple effect on the entire school, the athletic department in particular. Fewer than fifty-eight thousand people were at Camp Randall for the Illinois game. The department's finances were grim. By decade's end, a new chancellor, Donna Shalala, would hire a new athletic director—Pat Richter, a UW sports hero—and Richter would hire a new football coach, Barry Alvarez, who would soon make everyone forget the dark period of the late 1980s.

But for the band, other things happened during those years, many good, some less so.

In the 1989 season I welcomed the first-ever female drum major to the band. Deanna Willems—she went by Dee—had been the band's first female assistant drum major the year prior. She was a Waunakee High School graduate and a Spanish major at UW. She beat out five other candidates for the top job in 1989. Her style—all the drum majors have their own styles—used military moves but was graceful too. She had an outgoing personality and was a natural leader. The band was glad to have her, as was I.

Those with long memories might recall a controversy that developed for Ray Dvorak, when in 1947 a freshman from Menasha named Rosemary Schwebs volunteered herself as drum major for the band, spurred on by the men of Turner House on campus, who may have admired her appearance more than her baton twirling, though Schwebs had won a national drum majorette contest the year before. I came across her story while researching the centennial book.

"All I want is three minutes in the spotlight at one of the football games to do my stuff," Schwebs said. "Just so I can say I twirled for Wisconsin. I don't want Professor Dvorak to break any of his traditions, but I do want to do my stuff at least once."

Ray held firm, noting that he already had a drum major for 1947, and he was disinclined to break the tradition of male drum majors in any case. Madison newspapers picked up the controversy, which ceased when the UW administration invoked a rule prohibiting freshmen from engaging in extracurricular activities. Schwebs, however, was invited to perform at Carroll College's homecoming game against Ripon in Waukesha that November. Later, she served as drum major for the Green Bay Packers Lumberjack Band, performing in the Los Angeles Coliseum at halftime of a game between the Packers and the Los Angeles Rams.

In 2000, Schwebs gave an interview to the *Appleton Post-Crescent* recalling her attempt to be UW drum major in 1947.

"That was a big no-no," Schwebs said. "They never had a female majorette and probably never will."

The *Post-Crescent* needed a fact-checker: as noted, Dee Willems broke that barrier with our band in 1987.

~

More often than not, the newspapers were our friend, and this held true during the down years (for the football team) of the late '80s. When Pat Richter was named athletic director in 1989, *Washington Post* journalist Len Shapiro, a UW alumnus, came to Madison to write a story. He ended up writing about the band, with this lead for one of his pieces: "One of these days, the University of Wisconsin is going to field a football team that the Marching Band can be proud of."

One journalist took it to an extreme. Patrick Dorn was a former newspaper reporter returning to UW–Madison as an adult student in music education when he proposed writing a story for the University News Service about the band. The twist was that Patrick wanted to participate as a temporary band member for two weeks—he played clarinet— to really get a true feel for the band experience.

Because of the time he invested, Dorn's 1987 story—which was picked up by the *Sheboygan Press*, among other papers—did an exceptional job of conveying that experience. He wrote:

Leckrone is prone to temper tantrums and he had warned me I'd likely see at least one during two weeks of practice. I witnessed my first within the first 20 minutes. A general lack of attention and constant chattering among band members triggered the outburst.

"What is it with you people?" Leckrone screamed, disgustedly hurling his microphone to the ground. "Why do I have to go through this first practice after every show? You want all the fun, all the glory, but you don't want to put in the work. You don't know what it means to work. You're about one-third as good as you could be."

But come game day, Dorn noted, the band had done the necessary preparation, and the day's performances were successful. He ended his story with this:

> The band holds a special place in the hearts of Wisconsin fans who are not shy about showing their affection for the group or any individual in uniform. As the 200 of us locked arms to close the day with our own singing of "Varsity"—standing wet and dripping at the Humanities Building long after the game—the reason for the band's popularity suddenly seemed clear: Mike Leckrone manages every year to fashion a group that truly becomes family; one that embodies the spirit of UW–Madison's larger family of students, faculty, alumni and anyone else claiming to be a Badger backer.

Earlier in this narrative I mentioned a few of the pranks band members played on road trips. It happened at home, too, most often relatively harmless pranks, occasionally something more serious. Given a group of up to three hundred college students, it could hardly be otherwise. In Dorn's story he noted that at the end of one practice I gathered the band and relayed a story of some members who'd been involved in a scrape with the law during Homecoming week.

"Those involved in the incident sheepishly acknowledged it and apologized," Dorn wrote. "It was a difficult moment, but Leckrone turned it into a learning experience, reminding band members of their visibility on campus."

Dorn then quoted me: "We work too hard to draw attention to ourselves. We can't ask people to only notice us when we want them to. You owe it to yourselves and each other not to embarrass the group."

Alas, less than two years later we suffered an embarrassment when the *Wisconsin State Journal* wrote about a "band hymnal" that had been read by a member of the Wisconsin Student Association, who was greatly offended. I really couldn't blame her. As far as I know, most marching bands had similar "hymnals," which were filled with limericks of questionable taste and an occasional cartoon. It was usually put together leading up to a road trip, so people could read and maybe sing along during the trip. It was vulgar at times, no question. From what I'd heard on the trips, it was more scatological than sexually offensive, but I didn't see or hear everything. I probably should have paid more attention. The vulgarity was part of the charm for those who found it charming, and I can say that some of the women in the band were among the most enthusiastic contributors to the hymnal. Still, the publicity wasn't helpful. When I addressed it with the band, they understood, as they did in most similar situations. They never pushed back.

~

On a happier note, in 1988 our annual spring varsity band concert expanded to two nights. We'd been getting complaints from people who were unable to get tickets. Some of them were friends of band members, yet I had band members who were telling me, "We can't do concerts two nights in a row."

"Yeah, you can," I said.

Of course, we eventually wound up doing three nights in a row—Thursday, Friday, Saturday. What many people didn't realize is that we also had Wednesday dress rehearsal, so effectively it was four nights in a row. The band members learned how to negotiate that.

For the 1990 spring varsity band concert—two nights—we arranged a fifteen-minute *Phantom of the Opera* performance that was an expanded version of what we'd done during a football halftime at Camp Randall.

We often based one of our half-time shows on a Broadway musical. It probably started with *West Side Story*. I love musicals. At some point after we moved to Madison, Phyllis and I decided that as much as we liked the city, it would do us good to regularly get away for a few days. I came up with the idea of going to New York City and immersing ourselves in Broadway shows. I thoroughly enjoyed it. When our son moved to California, we adjusted our itinerary a bit. We'd start in New York, see several shows, and then fly to Las Vegas, where I would see more shows and Phyllis would reacquaint herself with the slot machines, which she got a kick out of. Then we'd fly to Los Angeles to see our son and enjoy the theater there.

Andrew Lloyd Webber, who, of course, did the score for *Phantom of the Opera*, is a favorite of mine. I really like the melodic content of everything he does. When you have a great melody, it makes it easy to write arrangements. And *Phantom* was hugely popular. The band kids knew about it before I brought it up. We tried to make our show as theatrical as possible.

For the Camp Randall *Phantom*, we had three trumpet players dressed identically as the Phantom, with the mask and cape and so forth. I stationed them so one was in the upper deck, one was in the end zone seats, and one was out on the field. Part of the show was that at some point, a solo trumpet would play, unamplified. People could still hear it and it was kind of spooky. I had one of the Phantoms pop up, play, and then be gone. Quickly, before he could have relocated, a second Phantom popped up, then a third. And everyone in the band wore the masks.

We did a similar thing at the varsity band concert. Different Phantoms showed up playing trumpet at various places in the Field House. We had a real organ and clips from the old Lon Chaney *Phantom* film. It was fun, and the most theatrical thing we'd ever attempted.

By the time we took the spring concerts to two nights in the late 1980s, my entrances had become a remarked-upon aspect of the shows and something we worked hard on to make special year after year. It really started even earlier. The second year of the concerts, when we were at Mills Hall in the Humanities Building, I ran down the steps from the back—from the top of Mills Hall to the stage. That was less common then than it is now, and people seemed to like it.

When we moved the shows to the Field House, the first year everything was so different that I decided on a conventional entrance. Things got rolling after that. Almost as soon as we finished the last show, we would start thinking about how I would make my entrance the next year. The stagehands had a lot to do with it. They'd make suggestions on what they thought they could pull off. It was fun to try to dream things up. Some of it, especially early, was so primitive I can't believe I did it. Silly too. I came in on a cow and on a cheese wedge and inside a Zamboni. The first time I "flew" in they had me in a harness, and all they could do was lower me down—I couldn't turn or move as I was able to do later. Another time they suspended a bicycle on a wire that ran the length of the basketball court. The bicycle was secured to the wire but the rider—me!—was not.

Still, when people would ask if I was ever scared, the answer was no, not during the entrance. But there was one time when I was spooked thinking about it afterward. We were in the Field House, and that year the stagehands told me they could run a fire pole—like firefighters use to slide down to their trucks—from the second balcony (or third level) of the Field House down to the floor. They said, "You just stand on the rail, grab the pole, and slide down." It didn't sound that dangerous, but there were no safeguards whatsoever, no way to rig a safety belt, and the pole was not directly adjacent to the second-balcony seating. I had to jump a small way from the rail to grab onto the pole. I didn't realize that until showtime. It's not as if we really practiced the entrances—there wasn't time or money for that. So I jumped and grabbed the pole. I told them after the show that it wasn't going to happen a second time.

It's also true that pyrotechnics was not the stagehands' strong suit. Sometimes it seemed they regarded gunpowder the way Paul Newman did playing Butch in *Butch Cassidy and the Sundance Kid* when he blew open a train car and nearly killed his entire gang standing nearby. I remember Robert (Sundance) Redford's wry reaction: "Think you used enough dynamite there, Butch?"

I should note that for the most part, the stagehands' judgment was sound. There was even a stagehand who twice became part of our show.

Frank Furillo, who was the lead singer of the popular Madison rock band The Rousers, often worked as a stagehand at our spring shows. We had a mutual friend in another stagehand, Bob Monschein, son of a School of Music colleague of mine. In a series of conversations it was decided that Frank would sing the Cab Calloway classic "Minnie the Moocher" during our varsity band concert. This was late '80s or early '90s and Frank was working the shows that year with the sound crew. When it was time, he snuck off, put on a purple zoot suit, and did a knockout "Minnie," even playing the song's horn intro on a harmonica. Nobody recognized him as one of the stagehands.

It went well enough that at the spring varsity concert in 1993—the same year the great bassist Richard Davis joined us—we arranged for Furillo to sing three Sinatra songs during the show. It came together quickly as those things often did, and I remember calling Frank just a few days before the concert and asking which songs he was going to sing. They were "The Best Is Yet to Come," "Summer Wind," and "Witchcraft." Frank later told a friend he was impressed I was able to arrange those songs as swiftly as I did.

We had fun with it the night of the show. At one point when the band finished a number, Frank appeared at the front of the stage wearing overalls and holding a microphone stand. He slammed it down in front of me.

"What are you doing?" I said.

"I'm getting ready for the Sinatra bit," Frank said.

My line then was, "What do you know about Sinatra?"

At which point a couple of students appeared and tore off Frank's (Velcro) overalls. He was wearing a dinner suit underneath. Someone in the front row tossed him a hat, and Frank shouted, "I'll show you Sinatra!" And he did, splendidly.

I think the band and I were a little taken aback when my School of Music colleague Richard Davis agreed to play at that 1993 spring concert. "Oh, yeah, I'll do that," Richard said, when I asked him.

It meant a lot to the kids. I told them they could find Richard's name on the back of some of the best jazz albums of all time. He'd played with most of the greats.

When we asked Richard what he wanted to play, he said, "Oh, we'll figure something out."

Basically, he asked me if we had anything in our catalog that was blues. My recollection is that we did, although I may have written something. Blues isn't especially difficult. Richard said, "Just play a little introduction and then I'll play." He said he'd give me a nod when he finished. He was such a terrific player on anything he tried. With us he played by the seat of his pants, which professionals are used to. It made the kids a little nervous, but it went fine.

What Richard did for us wasn't anything too intricate or showy, but just the fact that he was there, in our building, playing with us, meant a great deal. A true jazz legend. It was very gratifying.

I learned early there was no harm in asking people to play. Another musician who had played with the greats, longtime *Tonight Show* drummer Ed Shaughnessy, came to campus in fall 1990. Shaughnessy had played with Benny Goodman, Count Basie, Billie Holiday, and countless others. He was a big supporter of Very Special Arts and agreed to perform at halftime of the game in which our band played with the Very Special Arts Band. He also conducted a drum clinic at Mills Hall, with proceeds to Very Special Arts.

It was during that visit that I mentioned our spring varsity band concerts.

"We'd really like you to come and be a soloist," I said.

Shaughnessy said yes. It didn't happen immediately, but I think he came to campus three different times. He was a true professional and gentleman to work with, as nice and down-to-earth as any professional musician I ever met. He could be demanding, but never ridiculously demanding. He wanted things done the right way, but he also understood we were dealing with college kids who didn't have a lot of musical background. He was one of my favorite guest artists at the varsity band concerts, and it all started with me offhandedly asking if he'd consider it. Many people would have said, "Maybe we can work something out." Eddie said, "Sure, we'll make it happen."

Our special guests at the spring shows weren't always musicians. In April 1990, head coach Jeff Sauer and his Badger hockey team appeared on the heels of the rousing fifth national championship they'd secured in Detroit earlier that month. The crowd estimates at Joe Louis Arena were that fully half the fifteen thousand in attendance were Badger fans. New athletic director Pat Richter had found the money for a ninety-member contingent of the band to attend as well. We played a pep rally before the semifinal (a nail-biting 2–1 win over Boston College) and then the Badgers waylaid Colgate, 7–3, in the final.

People often speculate on which of the Badgers' numerous NCAA men's hockey titles was the greatest. For drama, it would be hard to argue against the first, in Boston in 1973. But many observers think the greatest college hockey *team*—Wisconsin or otherwise—was the 1977 Badger squad, which finished 37–7–1 and won the Big Ten, WCHA, and NCAA championships.

I'm fond of that 1977 championship team in part because the goal-tender, Julian Baretta, was a superstitious sort who asked if I could have the band play the famous Beatles song "Penny Lane" before the start of each period in games Baretta was goaltending. We did it, and as the song played Julian would skate backward from center ice into position in front of the Badger goal. I don't know what significance "Penny Lane" had for Baretta, but he said he also hummed the song to help him stay focused when the action of the game was at the other end of the rink.

After the 1990 championship game, some fifteen members of the band who hadn't made the trip to Michigan showed up at the Dane County airport that night to lead a crowd of well-wishers (five thousand by some estimates!) welcoming the victorious Badgers home.

⁓

It had been a great spring, but the season had a tragic conclusion.

On June 8, 1990, two four-year members of the band, Karl Unrein and Sherry Schoen, died in an automobile accident on US Highway 151 north of Sun Prairie. They were wonderful kids who had told me they were engaged and going to be married. Karl, who was from Waterloo, sang in a men's glee club quartet that performed at one of our spring concerts. He was going to come back for a fifth year in the band after spending the summer in Africa as part of his Fulbright scholarship. Karl triple majored in cultural history, African history, and African languages and literature. Sherry was from Kimberly and was studying for a degree in physical therapy. She played the frumpet—a combination of trumpet and French horn—in the band but could play other instruments, including piano, as well.

It was when Sherry was a junior at Kimberly High School that she first saw our UW Marching Band perform. The experience was transformative. Sherry's dad, Gilbert (Gib) Schoen, later told a reporter, "When she saw that band, she said, 'This is it. This is where I'm going to school and I'm going to get in the band.' She loved music."

Following the accident, both families established scholarship funds honoring Karl and Sherry. Karl's sister and brother-in-law, along with close friends, created the Karl John Unrein Memorial Scholarship. Gib Schoen and his wife, Donna, established the Sherry Schoen Memorial Scholarship, awarded annually to a Kimberly student who values and enjoys music, with no requirement that the student major in music in college.

Gib and Donna came to Madison for a Badger football game in fall 1991—their son, Scott, was then a freshman playing in our band—and they asked me if the band would consider coming up to Kimberly High School for a performance. I said we would and encouraged them to put in a formal request.

In March 1992, the band performed in the Kimberly High School gym, with proceeds going in part to the scholarship in Sherry's name. We did it annually for many years and we played at Waterloo High School, too, including a concert in 2010 on the twentieth anniversary of the accident. At those performances I always dedicated a song to Karl and Sherry.

seven

IF YOU WANT TO BE A BADGER

Starting in the late 1970s and continuing through the '80s, the band played at Edgefest, the annual late summer fundraiser for Edgewood High School in Madison. Edgefest started in 1973, and by 1979 we were opening the proceedings. Our involvement came through my friendship with my marching band predecessor, Ray Dvorak, who was a big supporter of Edgewood and lived not far from the school, on Jefferson Street. The band would meet at Camp Randall and then march down Jefferson Street, where we'd stop in front of Ray's house and play. We'd make sure his family knew we were coming so they'd have Ray—who turned eighty in March 1980—out on the porch to hear us. There's a great photo of Ray, his wife, Florence, and me on that porch with the band around us.

When Ray died in 1982, he was remembered as an "irreplaceable jewel" in a *Capital Times* editorial, which began, "If one man can be credited with elevating college band music nearly to the level of an art form, he is Ray Dvorak."

It took a decade, but in May 1992 the Raymond F. Dvorak Gallery opened in the lobby of Mills Hall in the Humanities Building on campus. It honored Ray and also served as a photographic history of the marching band. I worked with Jim Jordan, instrumental specialist with the School of Music, to make it happen. Jim and I shared an appreciation

Visiting with Ray and Florence Dvorak at their home. The band played for them before marching on to Edgefest. (UW Bands archive)

of history in general and music history in particular. He worked on the logistics—display cases and the like—and I gathered photos, some of which I'd already unearthed for the band centennial book.

We put one of Ray's uniforms in a display case not far from another that displayed a uniform of the famous 1915 marching band. Portraits of all past directors of the UW Marching Band were included. Florence and other Dvorak family members were at the dedication ceremony, along with Mary Lois Vega, daughter of W. T. Purdy, who composed the melody of "On, Wisconsin!"

Some faculty members in the School of Music looked askance at the gallery—an unfortunate reaction that occurred whenever the marching band received public attention. The fact is, Ray was faculty. He taught classes in arranging, conducting, and instrumental techniques.

Likewise, I taught classes throughout my UW–Madison career, in conducting, arranging, and a series of courses I really enjoyed called the History of American Popular Music.

When I was first hired, the course I was to teach was arranging. It turned out that I didn't like teaching it. I didn't enjoy grading papers, although I could have suffered through that. What really bothered me about the arranging class was that many of the students were not receptive to instruction. I'd give assignments, they'd turn them in, and I'd say, "Sorry, that's not going to work." Often the reply came back: "But that's what I *wanted* it to sound like." I'd say, "If you want it to sound terrible, you've succeeded." But they just weren't receiving the information that I'd spent a lifetime learning and refining. I had kids say, "You don't know what you're talking about." That attitude grew repugnant to me.

A School of Music colleague, Professor Bob Monschein—whose stagehand son I referenced earlier—had an office next to mine, and we were friendly. He knew songwriters and talked to me about Gershwin, Cole Porter, and others. I talked up Bix Beiderbecke and other players I admired. At some point, Bob recognized that I was looking for another class to teach. He was teaching one in American popular song and suggested I could teach a section of it. I did and called it the Big Bands, a course I really enjoyed. I felt I was offering something many had not heard about before, which was also true of the popular music history courses I taught. The course began with ragtime—circa 1915—and ended with the Beatles. I had students who hadn't heard of the Beatles and came up after class asking questions about them. I was amazed at how little some knew—but also how eager they were to learn.

With the big bands course, I usually reserved one lecture each semester to talk about Bix Beiderbecke. Why did I admire him so? Here was a young man who had no formal music training. He happened to have absolute pitch. What Bix could hear, he could play—on either piano or trumpet. In that sense he was in the genius category.

His ideas were fresh. If you hear a Bix Beiderbecke solo from 1928 and hear somebody else playing the same tune in 1938, it's the 1938 version that sounds dated. Bix had an ear for modern harmonies, and he was excellent at softening their dissonance. Bix had a way of voicing them so that they were there, but not dissonant, or impactful.

He was ahead of his time. In the manner of too many gifted musicians, he was also an alcoholic and died far too young, at twenty-nine. They've never made a truly good movie about his life. There's one starring Kirk Douglas called *Young Man with a Horn* in which Douglas plays a character named Rick Martin who was clearly inspired by Bix Beiderbecke. It's not terrible, but not great either.

Over the years people would ask me when I was going to do the "Bix lecture" so they might attend, even if they weren't in the class.

I did have fun with it. I'd take to that class a Bix Lives bumper sticker and paste it on a music stand for everyone to see. I set a photo of Bix on a pedestal, in memoriam. I pinned a red Bix Lives button on my shirt. Someone had given me a fan that had Bix's picture on it, so I used that too.

At some point in the Bix lecture, I would play a very lovely melody that I knew he had a big chorus on. I'd tell the class, "I just want you to listen to this before we talk about it. You're going to hear one of the immortals."

I'd put on the record and walk back and forth on the lecture stage as it was playing. Just before it got to the point where Bix came in, I'd stop walking, face the students, and proclaim: "It's time!"

At which point I ripped off the tearaway shirt I was wearing to reveal a second shirt underneath inscribed Bix Lives.

Did I mention I was a Bix Beiderbecke fan?

I taught other classes on the roots of rock and roll and one on legendary performers. It was fun for me to introduce students to people like Beiderbecke, Fats Waller, and so many others of whose importance they were unaware. I never allowed the classes to become too technical, because so many students in those classes weren't musicians. I tried to give them a feeling for all kinds of music. That's something I've preached all my life: Never feel as if there's only one kind of music that's any good. I told the kids my overflowing personal collection of records and books about music and musicians includes Bach, Beethoven, country, some rap, early and late blues—just about everything.

~

With teaching, the growth of the band department, and the marching band's increasingly high profile, by 1990 it was clear I was being pulled in too many directions and needed help. The position of assistant director of bands was created. It was a great help to me. The assistant director organized bands for women's athletic events, which were beginning to draw crowds. The assistant was responsible for a variety of administrative details and conducted a concert group for students who weren't music majors.

After a few years, the assistant was also given the job of percussion instructor—arranging and writing the material for the percussion section. Writing the drum parts for the band's arrangements had been one of the most laborious things I did. Drum parts have a lot of notes, and putting them down on paper is time consuming.

Having someone to bounce things off of was nice for me, as well—someone I could lean on if I was going to be late for a rehearsal or had some other conflict. The early assistant band directors, starting in 1990, were Enrique Feldman, Peter Griffin, and Galen Karriker, in that order. Galen could handle the drum assignment—I first met him at the 1993 Coca-Cola Bowl in Tokyo, when he was percussion instructor for the Michigan State band.

Having an assistant allowed me to concentrate on things I enjoyed and deemed most important, like football halftimes. We were always looking for new things to try at halftimes, and in the opening game of the 1991 season—against Western Illinois, September 14, at Camp Randall—we finally did something I had been thinking about for years.

A wedding.

It started when a Milwaukee businessman named Ken Werner, who was a rabid Badger football fan and equally devoted to the band, asked me if I could help him find a way to get married at halftime at Camp Randall Stadium.

Werner owned the I. M. Petite retail chain, and around Christmas 1990 he'd become engaged to Jill Dixon, his business partner, also a highly enthusiastic Badger fan. They'd been together a long time and had attended every home football game—and something like half the away games—for the past decade.

I told Ken I would check with the athletic department to see if it was OK. He wound up sending a video that convinced Pat Richter, the athletic director, that Ken and Jill were true Badger fans, and the department gave the go-ahead for the wedding.

"It might take some time out of your half-time performance," Ken said.

I didn't like hearing that. I said, "Why don't we use the wedding as our half-time show? You can get married on the fifty-yard line."

Everyone went all-in. The bride wore a white dress with red trim. The groom had a white tailcoat with a picture of Bucky Badger on the back, along with "Wisconsin" and "You've Said It All."

I thought I might officiate the wedding—like a captain on a ship— but I wasn't credentialed, and we wound up asking Dane County Judge

Angela Bartell, who had been a Badger cheerleader, to perform the ceremony.

For the music, we played "Get Me to the Church on Time" and "Love and Marriage," but then we mixed it up a bit and went back to the old English wedding tradition where the bride, to bring the marriage good luck, receives something old, something new, something borrowed, and something blue.

We played something old, Joplin's "The Entertainer"; something new, a new rendition of themes from the *New World Symphony*; something borrowed, Rossini's *William Tell Overture*; and something red (of course, rather than blue), "If You Want to Be a Badger."

Halftime concluded with the wedding ceremony. Ken and Jill rode in on the Bucky wagon, and Bucky Badger was the ring bearer. Judge Bartell pronounced them husband and wife. And then we played "Varsity." It was a most memorable halftime.

～

"If You Want to Be a Badger" and "Varsity" are two of what I consider to be the five songs that have iconic status for Badger fans and the UW Marching Band. You can likely guess two of the others: "On, Wisconsin!" and "You've Said It All." I've already described the genesis of "You've Said It All"—or at least how our band came to play it—and while I was researching the centennial book on the band, I learned the others also have interesting backstories. A band songbook had a bit of history on some of the songs, and Ray Dvorak's widow, Florence, gave me some historical material Ray had collected. Robert Gard and Arthur Hove have also explored some of the songs' origins in their books on Wisconsin.

The fifth song I consider quintessential for the band and our fans is called "The Touchdown Song" in the songbook. It's a variation on the turn-of-the-twentieth-century song "Hot Time in the Old Town Tonight" that was given a Badger twist by Philip Allen, an 1899 UW Law School graduate whose version concludes with the lyrics: "For when we hit their line / They'll have no line at all / There'll be a hot time / At Wisconsin tonight."

It's a great "fire-up" song. We played it before basketball tip-offs and hockey face-offs, and, especially, after the Badgers scored a touchdown at Camp Randall. Once the extra point was converted, we played "On, Wisconsin!" I was criticized by some for not playing "On, Wisconsin!" immediately after a score. But the "Hot Time" tradition was in place long before I arrived in Madison. My understanding is that early on, the students liked it and sang it after every touchdown. Ray Dvorak picked up on that and had the band play it. I kept up the tradition.

Certainly we played "On, Wisconsin!" at almost every opportunity, and I expect that will never change. It's the official school fight song *and* the official state song.

Early during my time in Madison, I was looking for a way to signal our last football half-time performance of the season. Something special to play near the end of halftime of the last Badger home game. At Butler, I used a song called "I'll See You in September," which made sense, but I didn't want to copy what I'd done at Butler.

What I came up with—and I was planning it for the end of only that one season—was to play a majestic preparation of "On, Wisconsin!" in a slow tempo. As we were playing it, the band moved into several horizontal lines. I planned it so that at the end of the piece, the band changed formation to spell "ON WIS." It made a big splash with the crowd. I felt I had my season closer, and from that point on, that was the way we closed every final home halftime. It was emotional for the kids—they knew it was the end. They really took to that closer, and it became such a highlight there was never a question of not doing it.

Once, however, it was nearly out of our hands. During the last home game in 1985, November 23 against Michigan State, snow fell and accumulated to the point that a UW official approached me and said we'd have to suspend our half-time performance so they could operate snowplows and keep the yard lines visible. I knew what being able to say a final goodbye meant to the band, so I lobbied for some kind of compromise and they finally acquiesced, saying we could play but the plows would be going too. I have a photograph from that afternoon and you can see the snowplows clearing off the yard lines at the sides of the field

The last home game of the 1985 season—the show must go on! (Gary Smith)

while we're performing in the middle. Everyone involved has a vivid memory of that day. Not only was it the last home game, there was also the drama of not knowing for sure whether we'd be able to go on.

A funny thing about "On, Wisconsin!": it was originally written for Minnesota by William T. Purdy, who in 1909 was hoping to win one hundred dollars in a contest for the best new University of Minnesota fight song. A friend of Purdy's, Carl Beck, was a UW graduate and convinced Purdy to use Beck's lyrics and tailor it to Wisconsin. As years went by, there were controversies over copyright, royalties, and even authorship—at one point Purdy's widow testily argued that Beck should not be listed as coauthor of "On, Wisconsin!" As for copyright, over time Paul McCartney and Michael Jackson were each reported as owning the song (by virtue of buying huge song catalogs), but "On, Wisconsin!" is now regarded to be in the public domain. I know we never asked anyone's permission to play it, and that never caused any trouble.

The ownership of "If You Want to Be a Badger" was never in question—it had distinctly UW roots—though its original title was "The Badger Ballad." The lyrics—which have been expanded over time—were written in 1919 by Julius E. Olson, a distinguished professor in UW's Department of Scandinavian Languages. Olson wrote it for an alumni dinner, and I particularly like that the music was arranged by

I had better luck riding this fiberglass cow than a real elephant at a Camp Randall halftime. (Gary Smith)

My grandparents, Glenna and Earl Heeter. (Leckrone family)

With my parents, Mary Louise and Harold "Leck" Leckrone, at a high school football game in Richmond, Indiana. (Leckrone family)

Directing the band at Camp Randall during my first season in Madison. (Leckrone family)

With a great friend, Elroy "Crazylegs" Hirsch. (Leckrone family)

The first time anyone rode an elephant into Camp Randall—and the last time. (Gary Smith)

Celebrating the Badgers' 6–0 win over Ohio State, their first win in decades in Columbus. (Gary Smith)

Directing the band at Camp Randall Stadium. White gloves were a trademark, and I wore a new pair every game. (Gary Smith)

The cow and me jumping over the moon at a UW Varsity Band concert. (Gary Smith)

Dueling with Bucky Badger: Somehow Bucky always won. (Gary Smith)

With J. J. Watt and my daughter Mika prior to J. J.'s UW commencement address. (Gary Smith)

With Darrell Bevell, prior to our induction into the UW Athletic Hall of Fame. (Gary Smith)

Celebrating in Camp Randall with UW alum Steve Miller, a UW band wannabe. (Gary Smith)

With Chancellor Donna Shalala in front of the boisterous band. (Gary Smith)

The band performed a half-time show on the flight deck of the USS *Nimitz*. (Gary Smith)

The final bow, of my final game, the Pinstripe Bowl at New York's Yankee Stadium. (UW Bands archive)

Marching through the arch on our way to Camp Randall Stadium was always an exciting prelude to the game. (Gary Smith)

A special moment, sharing the stage with members of my family at a varsity band concert. *From left*: Michael Mitmoen, Erik Leckrone, Raychel Wilson. To the right are David Jones and Grant Manhardt. (Gary Smith)

I'm too young to have great-grandchildren, but here they are, the Sanner kids: Apollo (*in front of me*) and Lyra standing behind her sister, Luna. (Leckrone family)

The entire Leckrone clan, with the exception of Luna, yet to be born. (Leckrone family)

Late for the group photo but treasured now: my great-granddaughter Luna. (Leckrone family)

I couldn't have done it without them: my last group of field assistants. (Gary Smith)

Celebrating my fiftieth anniversary as band director with family, Chancellor Rebecca Blank, and Athletic Director Barry Alvarez. (Gary Smith)

A pregame ritual: shaking hands with the band as they entered Camp Randall for my final game. (Gary Smith)

My final postgame Fifth Quarter at Camp Randall Stadium. (Gary Smith)

An oil painting gifted to me by the artist, Joy M. Hauser.

Charles H. Mills, the longtime director of the UW School of Music, for whom Mills Hall in the Humanities Building is named.

If you were to ask me my favorite circumstance of the band's playing "If You Want to Be a Badger," I think it would be when we performed it on the famous Santa Monica Pier one night during the run-up to the 1994 Rose Bowl. The lyrics, of course, reference "by the light of the moon," and as we played that evening a bright moon was above the Pacific Ocean. It was magical. I've mentioned how I believe it's important to consciously store moments of happiness in your memory bank. Playing "If You Want to Be a Badger" on the pier under that California moon was one.

Finally, and perhaps most enduringly, there's "Varsity." The tune was a Latin hymn by the French composer Charles Gounod that was given a Badger spin at the end of the nineteenth century by Henry Dyke Sleeper, a young instructor in the UW School of Music. Early on, Sleeper's song was alternately called "Toast to Wisconsin" and "Varsity Toast," then later shortened to "Varsity."

Ray Dvorak told me the story of how he introduced the now famous arm wave to the conclusion of "Varsity" soon after he arrived in Madison in the 1930s. Ray had been assistant band director at the University of Illinois and was in attendance when the Illini defeated the University of Pennsylvania in a hard-fought football game. Despite the tough loss, the Pennsylvania fans sang their school song at game's end and waved their hats back and forth as the song concluded. I'm not sure the hat aspect ever made it to Madison, but Ray introduced the arm wave, and it remains the emotional exclamation point on the time-honored "Varsity."

In the first chapter I mentioned the band's 1992 Seattle trip for the game against the University of Washington, noting that on the first day we were there we played on the USS *Nimitz* and at the Space Needle. I should also mention that on the second day we played on the Winslow Island Ferry, traveling across Puget Sound. The seascape was spectacular, and there was time for the band to take it in after our performance. The kids needed the rest because that night we played yet another show,

at the Westlake Center in the central city. The next day—game day—
the band played a pregame Badger Huddle for hundreds of Wisconsin
fans, performed (and earned two standing ovations) during halftime,
and stayed for a forty-five-minute Fifth Quarter after the final whistle.

We'd scraped to find the money for that trip—our first outside Big
Ten environs in years—and we made sure the band alumni and other
band friends who had helped us received their money's worth. It was
like a bowl game for the band. We left it all on the field—as they say in
sports—but when we were ready to fly home, our flight had a significant delay. By the time the plane was ready to load, there was only a
skeleton baggage crew to onboard the luggage. My assistant band director, Pete Griffin, some of the band staff, and I climbed into the baggage
compartment and started tossing suitcases in. It took a while. By time
we finished we were sweating and probably cursing. But when we got
to our seats, Pete and I just looked at each other and started laughing.
It was one of those things that certainly wasn't fun while it was happening but was already funny in retrospect. It was nine thirty when
we landed in Madison, and an hour later we were at the Humanities
Building for dismissal (a tradition from our Big Ten road trips) singing
"Varsity" and climbing on the Humanities wall, facing Park Street—the
kids, not me—something I doubt the administration appreciated.

One thing the 1992 Seattle trip did—apart from prepare us for the up-
coming Japan and Rose Bowl adventures—was make clear that the band
needed a financial backstop, a source of funds if unexpected opportunities, such as travel, presented themselves. We also lacked in our annual
budget sufficient funds to save for new instruments or new uniforms,
which inevitably we would need.

After Seattle, prominent alumni businessmen Jere Fluno and Jim Burt,
along with other Badger alumni, met with me to discuss how we might
address the funding issue. They suggested establishing an endowment
fund through the UW Foundation. The "Spirit of Wisconsin" campaign
was launched in spring 1993 with a goal of raising $3.3 million.

In the end, the goal may not have been ambitious enough—over time inflation can take big bites out of a set return. Still, the endowment was important for us, and much appreciated. Eighteen months after we began, I was handed—at halftime of a football game at Camp Randall Stadium—a check for $1.1 million, which meant we'd already made it to one-third of our fundraising goal.

I was pleased, as well, that the publicity around the endowment let the public know a bit about the band's finances. I believe many people were surprised to read a *Wisconsin State Journal* editorial that began with this:

> The University of Wisconsin Marching Band neither sounds nor looks like an outfit that lives on a shoestring budget. The band's 288 members march seamlessly, play gloriously and always appear crisp in their uniforms, no matter what the weather at Camp Randall Stadium.
>
> The band has always looked like a million bucks . . . Looks are deceiving. The band's operating budget is about $83,000 for this year, nearly half of which is raised at the band's spring concert. The UW athletic and music departments provide some financial support, but not much. In fact, the UW Marching Band's budget is smaller than any other marching band budget in the Big Ten or Pacific Ten conferences.
>
> No wonder people use the phrase "we belong to everyone, yet no one" to describe the band.

The *State Journal* urged people to contribute to the endowment. One way we encouraged donations was an "adopt a member" program that allowed donors to sponsor someone in the band. It was a bit of a gimmick because the money went into the general endowment fund, but it allowed the donor to feel connected and the kids they sponsored were benefiting. It was basically the cost of an instrument. The amount for endowing a cymbal player, for instance, was $3,000 (in the early 1990s), while a sousaphone player was $9,000. Tubas were the most expensive and yet went the fastest because—there's no accounting for taste—everyone loved the tubas. For a time, we had donors join us on the field during a game at Camp Randall.

Another thing we did to raise money—which began long before the endowment but continued into the '90s and beyond—was what I called "run-out" concerts at high schools, mostly but not all in Wisconsin. Our first was at Oak Creek High School, south of Milwaukee. It turned out very well. They'd advertised the concert—we did our sit-down show—and paid our expenses. The Oak Creek band parents spread the word, and it wound up being a good fundraiser for their band. High school bands were often struggling for funds in those days, and I suspect it's still true today.

We started playing at schools in other cities—Sheboygan, Racine, Beaver Dam, many more—and began to regard the concerts as an opportunity to both showcase the band and make some money. From a public relations standpoint, the adults in attendance would observe the show and often conclude the Wisconsin band kids were a pretty terrific bunch. They'd talk us up afterward. Then, too, we began to contract with the host schools so our band would get at least a portion of the profits from ticket sales for the shows. We worked out a split, generally around 50–50. The high school band programs would still profit as well. As our popularity grew, some of those performances amounted to $5,000 or $6,000 going both ways. We'd bus over and the school would often put out a buffet meal, which my kids appreciated because they could eat as much as they wanted. Eventually we were doing eight or ten run-out concerts a year.

~

When our endowment fund was announced in spring 1993, nobody knew that fall would bring a football season unlike any in the history of Badger athletics. We did know that the last regular-season game of the year would be played against Michigan State in the Coca-Cola Bowl in Tokyo, which took the band—seventy members, anyway—to Japan on a trip I mentioned in chapter 1. It's funny about that trip. Had it occurred in any other year, it would have been a huge deal, a lifetime memory. But if you ask the band kids about it today, many will smile and nod and begin talking about the Rose Bowl, which followed.

My Tokyo memories start before the '93 football game, when that summer I attended a meeting in New York City with the Japanese organizers of the Coca-Cola Bowl. They flew both me and my Michigan State counterpart to New York, and we met in a fancy hotel conference room overlooking the East River. It frankly wasn't much of a meeting. They spoke a bit about how long we'd be playing and the music they wanted us to play. They gave me a CD with that music and noted we'd be playing with Ninja, the boy band. And they gave me a boom box, which was unwieldy to take home on the plane but which I still have all these years later.

Back in Madison, we settled on seventy as the number of band members we could take on the Tokyo trip. But by the time we reached the tail end of the '93 football season, it was clear the Badgers would also be going to a bowl game after Japan: the Rose Bowl, if we beat Michigan State, though even with a loss in Tokyo, the Badgers would get a bowl bid. As a result, after the last home game, against Illinois, I had to rehearse two bands, one with seventy members and one with all two hundred–plus.

There was also a great deal of administrative work in advance of the Tokyo trip. We were in frequent contact with the athletic department about what was and what wasn't allowed. We needed to arrange passports and catalog and weigh all our equipment. Our band uniforms were packed in cartons per specific instructions, and I was nervous because we never saw them once we landed in Japan. In fact, we didn't see them until about an hour before our performance, when a truck arrived carrying the uniforms.

I noted that in the two weeks between the Illinois game and our trip to Tokyo, we'd tried to follow the football team's example and adjust our body clocks to Japan time. It didn't work as well for us because of our various schedules, but we tried, nevertheless. And we all participated in a class that explained Japanese customs and traditions, and how to conduct ourselves as guests. Part of that dealt with Japanese cuisine, although, once we were there, our hosts insisted on providing hot dogs and Kentucky Fried Chicken at just about every meal.

One thing that was different in Tokyo was our practice facility. We arrived at Narita Airport, one of two international airports serving Tokyo, a little after midnight on December 1—the game was scheduled for December 5 (December 4 back in Wisconsin). It meant we'd have at least three days of practice for what was being billed as a traditional pregame show and a five-minute half-time performance.

The place they had for us to practice was an indoor baseball diamond, baseball being very popular in Japan. It was not ideal for a marching band. The lighting was poor, and there was an elevated pitcher's mound and next to no ventilation. Early on we kicked up so much dust from the field's basepaths that we had to stop and ask them to sprinkle the infield with water.

The other issue was a bowl official who was present at rehearsal and making a big deal out of having a stopwatch to make certain we didn't exceed the five minutes allotted our half-time performance. I knew we'd been running long in practice. Part of that was having to prepare both the seventy-member and the two-hundred-member bands back in Madison.

I resolved this at the Tokyo rehearsal by telling the band we were going to march and play at an extremely fast tempo.

"It's not how we'll actually perform it," I said.

The bowl official was staring at his watch and didn't note the frenzied tempo. He looked up from his watch at the five-minute mark and we'd finished. He gave me a grin and a thumbs up. He didn't notice that my band members—who were in good shape—were bending over, hands on knees, gasping as if they'd been doing wind sprints.

The night before the game there was an official welcoming banquet in a huge ballroom where we finally dined on some authentic Japanese dishes. We'd also had a sightseeing tour during which we saw the Imperial Palace and visited a Shinto shrine where a wedding was taking place. The shrine had a beautiful botanical garden and, near the entrance to the shrine's innermost grounds, flowing water in which a purification or cleansing ritual called *temizuya* may be performed by washing one's hands. Band members were invited to participate, and since tradition also allows visitors to make a wish, seventy appeals for "Badgers to the Rose Bowl" were likely issued almost simultaneously.

That wish, of course, was granted.

~

Although I touched on some of the highlights of the long-awaited trip to Pasadena in chapter 1, I want to share a few more Rose Bowl memories.

It is not widely known outside of our family that I came close to not going to the Rose Bowl at all.

The annual Midwest Band Clinic was held in Chicago in December 1993, just a couple of weeks before the Rose Bowl. I always liked to attend and felt especially compelled this time because there would be a meeting of the Big Ten band directors, and I'd be able to ask all of them where they planned on being on New Year's Day. They knew where I was going to be—in Pasadena!

We usually carpooled to the clinic, but I had to stay back a day in Madison to attend to some Rose Bowl trip details. I set out for Chicago by myself on December 17. I was on Interstate 90 in Illinois, some-where around Belvidere, and about to pass a semi. The truck was in the right lane, and I was approaching from behind in the left lane. A car was behind the truck in the right lane, and suddenly—I must have been in his blind spot—the driver of that car pulled out sharply to the left, intent on passing the truck himself. I was sure he was going to hit me, and I swerved hard to the left. Our cars didn't collide, but my car rolled over and ended upside down in the median strip.

It happened in an instant. I remember my exact thought: "Now I'm never going to get to the Rose Bowl."

In reality, although it was frightening, I wasn't badly injured. The only lasting remnant is a small scar on my wrist that happened when I undid my safety belt, not thinking through that I was hanging upside down. Gravity got me. I dropped and cut my wrist. The other casualty was my shoes. Traffic was stopped and someone called an ambulance. Somewhere between the ambulance arriving and dropping me at the hospital, I lost my shoes.

A story that lives in Leckrone family folklore concerns a phone call I made from the hospital and its aftermath. I knew not to call my wife at home. Phyllis was bowling that day. She was serious about it and participated in at least two leagues. So instead, I called my daughter Mika and told her what had happened.

"I'm OK," I said. "Tell your mother, but don't upset her. You'll need to get her and drive down here to the hospital and pick me up because my car is totaled."

At the bowling alley, Mika said, "Mom, don't worry. Dad's fine. But he's been in a car accident in Illinois and we have to go get him."

"OK," Phyllis replied, after a pause. "But first I have a couple more lines to bowl."

She really enjoyed bowling.

One enduring memory, once we made it to Pasadena, is the amazing pep rally that was held at the ABC Entertainment Center, across the street from the Century Plaza hotel in Century City, where the Wisconsin Alumni Association had booked a thousand rooms for Badger fans. The rally was the afternoon of Thursday, December 30, and Rose Bowl officials were later quoted saying they'd never seen anything like that Century Plaza pep rally. I'm not good at crowd estimates—they varied between ten thousand and thirty thousand—but the place was *packed*. We shared a tiny stage with speakers who included Governor Tommy Thompson, Chancellor David Ward and former Chancellor Donna Shalala, and Pat Richter, the athletic director who had starred in the last Badgers' Rose Bowl in 1963 and made this one possible when he hired Barry Alvarez as head football coach.

An Eau Claire *Leader-Telegram* columnist noted the next day that the speakers "played only supporting roles for the main attraction—the Badger band."

He continued: "[It was] an endless sea of red and white. The colorful sea came complete with the feeling of waves because the dancing, jumping, gyrating crowd caused the concrete surface over an underground parking ramp to shake noticeably."

It was a pep rally for the ages.

The next morning was our last rehearsal. We were one day away from the parade and the game that would be watched by tens of millions of people. I didn't want to add to any nerves the kids might be feeling, so I wasn't unduly serious. I did, however, make one point that perhaps they hadn't considered amid all the hoopla of the week. Along with, as always, representing the university and the state of Wisconsin, I reminded them that tomorrow they would be standing on the shoulders of all the University of Wisconsin Marching Band members who had come before them and would have given anything to perform at a Rose Bowl. I said they owed those predecessors their very best. I think it resonated.

I mentioned in the opening chapter how grueling the Tournament of Roses Parade could be for a band. After all, the parade route is more than five miles long. Some other band directors suggested—and we implemented—a plan in which after the first half hour of the parade, once we were past the television cameras, some of the band members alternated lip-synching their parts. While pretending they were playing, they could catch their breath. Given the tight proximity the parade required, it really didn't matter if 250 or 150 were playing at any given time. The break helped, the players appreciated it, and I did the same thing at subsequent Rose Parades. Another parade tradition that they appreciated—and I did too—was the stand that a famous fast-food chain in California, In-N-Out Burger, set up for us to visit when the parade was over.

I walked with the band in the front right corner during the parade. My primary responsibility was to signal, with hand signs we'd developed, to the drum major so he'd know when to play. We played constantly for the first thirty minutes, a little less so after that. People along the parade route were always calling for us to play. We played a lot, but we had a football game that afternoon to perform at as well. I shook many hands during the parade—there were people in red everywhere with big smiles and arms extended. It was more fun than I anticipated.

Some fans have asked about the song I chose to close our rock and roll–themed half-time show. We'd called the show "Early Rockers," and we'd rocked the Rose Bowl by the time we were almost finished. In thinking earlier about an ending, I knew I wanted something majestic, and honestly, rock and roll songs really aren't majestic.

I chose "My Way," a song that almost everyone knows. We noted that while it isn't a rock and roll song, Elvis Presley, the King of Rock and Roll, often closed his concerts with it. We said we'd like to do the same thing, and it worked.

Unsaid, but in the minds of many in the band, there was another reason to end this historic half-time performance with "My Way."

By the early and mid-1990s, our band had been on the receiving end of numerous accolades—in early 1993, for instance, *Playboy* magazine named the UW band the best in the country. There had been numerous other honors.

But we'd also been criticized in some quarters, by people who said our performances were undisciplined, not dignified in the marching band tradition.

Fair enough. Everyone is entitled to an opinion.

We knew who we were, and it showed in all our performances that week in Pasadena, from Disneyland to the Santa Monica Pier and the Century Plaza, from the Rose Parade right up to that last song during halftime.

We did it our way.

eight

MOMENTUM AND LOSS

The energetic euphoria generated by the first-ever Rose Bowl win and the incredible week in California surrounding it carried over once we were back home.

There were parties and tributes, none complete—or so we were told—without at least a partial band presence. One that was special happened in Milwaukee on January 6, when Vice President Al Gore, former Wisconsin Congressman Les Aspin, Donna Shalala, Barry Alvarez, and twelve members of the winning Badgers' team appeared at a tribute rally at Washington High School. Gore claimed honorary Badger status by pointing out his mother had attended UW Law School. They all either danced with Bucky or helped "conduct" the band. Rose Bowl MVP Brent Moss presented Shalala, who had left campus to become Health and Human Services secretary under Gore's boss, President Bill Clinton, with an array of Badger gear, which I doubt she was short on after several years as chancellor. It was a celebration where nobody could seem to stop smiling, the band included.

The football team's success carried across the major sports as the year progressed. The men's basketball team made it to the NCAA tournament for the first time since the 1940s. Wisconsin's first- and second-round games were in Ogden, Utah, and when I arrived Thursday, the day of the Badgers' opener against Cincinnati, I was told by Cheryl Marra,

an assistant UW athletic director, that Stu Jackson, the UW head basketball coach, was upset about band members partying post-midnight
in the hotel the night before. My assistant band director, Pete Griffin,
and about thirty members of the band had arrived in Utah Wednesday
night. When I looked into it, I became convinced the partiers who
upset Jackson were not band members. Pete had been in contact with
the hotel front desk until very late, with no complaints. Still, I wasn't
there, I can't be certain. Our exuberant style in performance was what
so many loved about us; toning down that exuberance once the instruments were put away was something we stressed and did our best to
address. Utah wouldn't be the last time.

Regardless of what happened that Wednesday night, Jackson's Badgers
beat Cincinnati on Thursday, 80–72. UW was knocked out in the next
round by Missouri, but making the tournament was a sign a Badger basketball renaissance had begun. Men's hockey, meanwhile, had another
fine year in 1994, making it to the semifinals of the Eastern Regionals,
where they lost to Boston University, 4–1.

For the band, the Rose Bowl enthusiasm carried over into our 1994
spring concert season, and for the first time we added a third night to
our varsity band concert at the Field House. We hadn't really planned
to do three, but due to the Rose Bowl momentum, our first two nights
sold out almost as soon as the tickets became available. The production
crew really convinced me about a third night. They said there's little difference in setting up the stage so it's ready for Thursday in addition to
Friday and Saturday. There's not much extra expense beyond hiring
ushers for another night.

I do remember someone asking, "Can the band do three nights?"

"They can if I say they can," I said.

As I've noted, three nights really meant four, because we had a dress
rehearsal Wednesday night. The first few rehearsals were little more than
talking through what would happen, but as the shows grew more com-
plicated, the stage crew required a full dress rehearsal for things like lighting cues.

That fall, the band debuted new uniforms at the Homecoming game in October against Minnesota. In a way, that was a product of the Rose Bowl as well. We were very much on display in Pasadena, and at one point during that week we had to send the uniforms out to be cleaned, to help them look less worn. We resolved to replace them. I didn't change much in the design. The big difference was the front shield. It had been red with a black emblem in the middle. I changed that emblem to white. I thought it stood out more.

$\sim$

The year that began on such a high note with the Rose Bowl win ended in tragedy. On the afternoon of Tuesday, December 13, I received a phone call from Mike Dibble, a paramedic with the Madison Fire Department. I'd known Mike since he was a standout goaltender with the UW hockey Badgers in the 1970s. Mike was calling to tell me Jack Rane had just suffered a fatal heart attack.

I rushed to Jack's West Side apartment, but Mike met me at the door and counseled against going inside. There was nothing to be done. Jack was just fifty. He was a Madison native and an Edgewood High School graduate who had heart trouble in his family. He'd had a heart attack, and quadruple bypass surgery, five years earlier.

Mike Dibble called because he knew Jack and I were close. Jack loved the Badgers and especially the band. I sometimes referred to him as an unpaid assistant, but that hardly did justice to all the ways he helped out over the years. His personality? A character, a wheeler-dealer who occasionally went over the top, but a good soul. The band liked him very much and so did I.

Early on, just after Badger men's hockey had moved to the Dane County Coliseum and Bob Johnson had convinced me to take the varsity band to the games, Jack asked to sit in on some songs. It was somewhat ragtag in those early hockey days, and Jack could play bass drum. No harm in him sitting in. He especially liked "And Then There's Maude," the theme song to a 1970s CBS sitcom, and playing it with him became a tradition at the hockey games. We'd play it right before the Badgers came out of their dressing room and then move to "On, Wisconsin!" when the skaters hit the ice.

Over time Jack helped me by organizing the high school band days during football season; he helped sell tickets to the spring varsity band concerts in the days before it was so wildly popular; and he helped initiate a popular line of UW band memorabilia, including clothing. Jack worked at the Hub, a men's clothing store, and brokered a good deal for us.

Jack started announcing for the band at Camp Randall in the early 1970s, and in the mid-1980s he became the public address announcer for football and basketball. At the basketball games he and I had almost a telepathy when there was a stoppage in play. He'd give me one kind of look when he was going to make an announcement and another when it was OK for us to play.

Many people feel Jack's finest hour came after the Michigan game in 1993 when the fans rushed the field at Camp Randall. He stayed calm and instructed people over the public address to do likewise. He was shaken by it, as we all were, but he rose to the occasion that day.

When Dibble called me with the news that Jack had died, there was a band practice later that afternoon. I waited until the end of rehearsal to tell the kids because I knew Jack would have wanted it that way. Usually there's enthusiasm at the end of a practice, but there was a shocked silence when I delivered the news. I'd never heard it that quiet. Even the freshmen who were just getting to know Jack knew the history of what he'd meant to the band.

There was a basketball game at the Field House two nights later. It felt empty without Jack. We played "And Then There's Maude" in his honor.

When Jack died, we needed a new announcer for the band at Camp Randall. The role was assumed by someone whose history with the band went back two decades. John Biester started with the band as a freshman tuba player in 1973. The next year he became drum major, a position he held for four years. That is unlikely to ever happen again—

underclassmen typically have trouble gaining the respect from the older kids that a drum major needs. But John was a very good drum major with a maturity beyond his years. It didn't hurt that he also had a physical presence. He was a big, tall guy who might have played football.

John eventually rejoined our band as a field assistant. When Jack Rane died, John took over as band announcer, and as I write this, he's approaching three decades in that role. John is also band director at Parker High School in Janesville.

Some people might think announcing for the band is easy, just letting the crowd know what song is coming next. But after twenty years as announcer, John wrote a piece for the Wisconsin Alumni Association that gave a little better sense of what's involved. He noted that I'd give him a script of the show, usually on Thursday, and then he would come to our early Saturday morning rehearsal (after a 6 a.m. breakfast at Mickie's across the street).

John wrote: "Rehearsal is my one chance to get the timing down for my script and make note of Mike's actions. It is when I get both musical as well as visual cues. . . . Where is the break? How many seconds do I have? Should I wait until later in the vamp to start? It used to be I got two run-throughs at each rehearsal. This last season, each show was one time. Maybe Mike thinks I finally have the hang of this? Nah, he's just messing with me."

Less than a year after Jack Rane's fatal heart attack, our band family suffered another terrible loss. Kurt Mullendore, who played trombone in the band and then served as a highly popular field assistant, took his own life in September 1995. It was all the more shocking because Kurt was so jovial on the outside. He loved playing the accordion he inherited when his dad died. He played it on the beach in Santa Monica at the Rose Bowl and then at the hotel in Tampa—repeated renditions of "In Heaven There Is No Beer"—at the Hall of Fame Bowl in January 1995.

At the time of his death, Kurt had gone back to school at UW–La Crosse, studying to be a band director. He'd have been a good one. He had a kid-like quality he never lost, and young people could relate to him. You can look for answers when something like Kurt's death happens, but real answers are rare. It's just sad. Bill Garvey, the McFarland High School band director, had a photo on his wall of himself, Kurt, and Jack Rane at the '94 Rose Bowl, all with hats turned backward, faces joyful. Less than two years later, two of the three were gone.

~

In September 1996, the football Badgers were making a return trip to Las Vegas for the first time in a decade, but it appeared the band might not be able to go along. This made neither the band nor the Badger fans happy. I remembered our last Vegas trip, in 1986, which I mentioned in chapter 6 and commemorated by framing a Las Vegas newspaper article headlined "UW Band—The Best Show in Town."

Not bad being the best show in town—in Las Vegas.

That year they had closed some blocks on Fremont Street downtown—notoriously known as Glitter Gulch—for us to play, and our fans mobbed the street.

A few months before the 1996 game, after news stories appeared about there being no budget for the band to make the trip, I came up with the idea of having the band play shows in Vegas and charging—modestly, ten or fifteen dollars—for tickets to cover our expenses.

Not all my ideas over the years succeeded, but that one did. We played three concerts at the famed Stardust Hotel. Red-clad Badger fans were everywhere. The game drew more than forty thousand people, breaking the record for the largest crowd to see an event of any kind in Nevada. The previous record of thirty-nine thousand was held by the Grateful Dead.

In 1986, the University of Nevada, Las Vegas, upset the football Badgers, but this time Wisconsin won going away, 52–17. We played a Fifth Quarter, which is not always welcome away from Camp Randall. The Vegas officials loved it because it spread out the crush of traffic heading from the stadium to the Strip.

We made a third trip with the football team to Las Vegas in 2002, and it wound up being one of the strangest games in all my years with the band. Game day was August 31, and it was the season opener for UNLV. The Badgers, however, had opened the season a week earlier at Camp Randall with a 23–21 victory over Fresno State. Having a game under their belts was a big advantage for the Badgers, yet the opening betting line had Wisconsin favored by only three points. As the week went on, the line was eventually pushed to six—it meant a great many people were betting on the Badgers—but even at six points, savvy fans arriving in Las Vegas from Madison couldn't get to the sports books fast enough to bet on Wisconsin.

For nearly three and a half quarters, it looked as if Wisconsin fans were going to cash in huge. With 7:41 to go in the game, the Badgers led, 27–7. The point spread was easily covered. Badger fans were smiling, breathing easy, wondering how best to spend their winnings.

But then the stadium lights went out.

It wasn't total blackness, but it was dark enough, and nobody knew what the heck was going on. The game was stopped, of course, and then someone from the UW athletic department came up to where I was sitting with the band in the south end zone and asked if we could play while game officials tried to get more information.

"We don't know how long this will last," he said.

I said, "Well, we have all the Fifth Quarter stuff memorized, so we could play for a half hour if you need us to."

We probably played for ten minutes, at which point someone came up and told me they'd declared the game over and we should begin getting the band out of the stadium.

Wisconsin was declared the winner of the game, but in the aftermath the real drama involved the gambling. The Nevada gaming commission had allowed betting on UNLV and other Nevada team games only since February 2001. And the gaming rules in Las Vegas held that for a college game to count officially for gambling purposes, fifty-five minutes (of the scheduled sixty) must be played.

In other words, the UW–UNLV game was 2:41 short of counting. It was taken off the books; bettors would get the amount of their bet back and no more.

Badger fans were outraged. Conspiracy theories sprouted. What had caused the power outage? Had the powerful casinos, about to lose big on the game, somehow staged the blackout? There were rumors of cars running into electrical boxes and other bookie-inspired mischief.

The official explanation, such as it was, blamed an old-fashioned equipment failure about a mile and a half from the stadium. There was apparently no one on the grassy knoll in Las Vegas, although some Badger fans remain skeptical.

~

We had a little Vegas sizzle—or show business pizzazz, anyway—at our varsity band concert in spring 1997. We'd be moving to the new Kohl Center in April 1998, so we titled the show "Farewell to the Field House." Tom Wopat, a Wisconsin native who had become both a star on TV and Broadway and a good friend of mine, helped us close out at the Field House.

I'd known Tom, who was originally from Lodi, since he was a student at UW–Madison. We arrived on campus the same year, 1969. Tom was a vocal performance major and not officially in our marching band. Soon after Tom arrived in Madison, he approached me, introduced himself, and said, "You know, I play a little trombone. Can I sit in with the varsity band sometime?" He'd played with his high school band, and I said sure, why not? He sat in with us several times. I think he liked that carrying his trombone case got him into the basketball games. Tom was a big basketball fan. Decades later, in 2014, I was getting on the bus to go to the airport in Texas after Kentucky beat the Badgers in heartbreaking fashion at the buzzer of a Final Four semifinal. My cell phone rang. It was Tom, calling to commiserate.

His real talent, of course, was singing—and acting, too, as it turned out. I think early on he wanted to be a rock and roll singer, but his voice teacher told him all that shouting could damage his voice.

Tom gained stardom when *The Dukes of Hazzard* became a hit on CBS television. It didn't change our relationship. He performed at the spring varsity band concert for the first time in 1980 while *Dukes* was still on the air, and he returned numerous times, including the April 1997 "Farewell to the Field House" performance. He never asked for any compensation beyond a room at the Edgewater. When I was inducted into the University of Wisconsin Athletic Hall of Fame in 2017, Tom came to the ceremony at Union South. I know that more recently he ran into some legal trouble, but it couldn't temper my appreciation for all he did for us.

～

In May 1997, the month after our last Field House show, I was asked to give a Founders' Day speech by the UW–Madison Alumni Club of Sheboygan County. It was at the Sheboygan Yacht Club, and as the *Sheboygan Press* reported the next day, it "drew record attendance."

I didn't mind doing those events when my schedule allowed. Alumni clubs around the world hold Founders' Day fundraisers annually from February to May in honor of the first UW–Madison classes, which were held in February 1849. Let's face it: They make a pretty easy audience. Everyone already loves the Badgers!

With me, they generally just wanted to hear band stories. In Sheboygan, I told some funny tales and had everyone laughing, but then I added that being in the band requires more hard work and commitment than some people realize.

"When the temperature is twenty-five degrees," I said, "and rain is changing to sleet, and fifty-mile-per-hour winds develop, I tell band members to be tough enough to eat a rock."

The "eat a rock" mantra for the band dated to the early 1980s. I generally try to give an emotional pep talk the night before a big performance—say, the night before a football Saturday—and on the night I'm remembering I wasn't completely satisfied with the work ethic I'd been witnessing. I felt I needed to fire them up. I talked about what I wanted to see the next day, and I said, "When you go out there tomorrow, you need to be tough enough to eat nails."

I paused, and added, "No, you need to be tough enough to eat a rock!"

It was hardly out of my mouth when the band started chanting: "Eat a rock! Eat a rock! Eat a rock!"

In Indiana and down through Appalachia there is an old saying, "Root hog, or die." It basically means "sink or swim," and it dates to the time of free-range hogs that had to root up food to eat. I felt we might have something similar, something that would resonate, with "eat a rock."

We started adapting the slogan for different things. We put it on T-shirts and bumper stickers. Eventually I even had a little plaque made and asked Otto Breitenbach—then a top UW athletic administrator—if he cared if I cemented it to the stadium at the ramp that goes down to the field from the Camp Randall interior. He gave us the OK. It's supposed to be the last thing the band sees before they hit the field. We made quite a ceremony of putting it up there.

As time went on I was always trying to find other mottos. I came across one—"The will to win is nothing without the will to prepare"—that I really liked. It's what I was trying to teach the band. I changed it to "The will to succeed is nothing without the will to prepare" and had some T-shirts made up for the band. It made zero impact. It turned out the quote has been attributed to numerous coaches and may even have been used in an athletic gear commercial. It was shopworn, and the band yawned.

I said, "Well, OK, come up with something yourselves."

They put their heads together and came up with "Pain is temporary, pride is forever." I liked it and we adopted it. I've seen it since as a motto elsewhere, but I'd never seen it before they proposed it.

Shortly after I returned from my speech in Sheboygan, I received a call from a reporter at the *Tampa Tribune* who was pretty excited about a Florida saxophonist and entrepreneur who had patented an "instrument warmer" he thought might help bands who play outdoors in cold weather. The reporter was calling to ask me about the product, which had a heating element inside an insulated cover for use with a wind instrument. It would be powered by a battery pack attached to a musician's belt.

I was gracious to the reporter—I said we'd take a look—but the truth is I was always getting approached by so-called entrepreneurs trying to sell me on their "revolutionary" inventions. I remember one guy who thought he'd solved the problem of trumpet players worrying about applying too much pressure to the instrument. He had devised a mouthpiece that had some kind of spring in it, so if you pressed too hard on it, the air would come out the side of the mouthpiece. In other words, if you pressed too hard, you couldn't get a sound. But no trumpet player is going to want that because they could be in the middle of a show unable to make music. It was impractical in my opinion, as was the heating element–battery pack idea.

$\sim$

Moving our spring varsity band concerts to the Kohl Center, in April 1998, was a big deal. I said we had to put on a great show to make people forget there was no place to park—but then, it wasn't exactly easy to park around the Field House, either.

My immediate feeling about the Kohl Center as a venue was that it opened up possibilities. At the Field House, we had to manufacture anything extraordinary we wanted to do. At the Kohl Center—just one example—we had lifts that went up and down. The stagehands didn't have to do everything by hand.

It just felt more professional. There was a sense that this was the big time. And each year we added to it. TV monitors enabled me to watch as the show was going on. One was right in front of me, and others were on either side of the stage. If I needed to see something, I could. I was constantly in touch with the production crew. There were times when I'd be conducting and a voice in my ear said, "Mike, we're going to need a little more time. We're not ready for the next bit. Can you stretch a little?" You had the feeling you were really in the entertainment business, and I think the band felt it too.

It was all to the good, but it took some getting used to. We built a long catwalk off the main stage that had a small stage at the end of it. That's where we set up "Westside Andy" Linderman, one of our guest

artists that first year in the Kohl Center. Andy is a terrific Madison-
based musician, a blues harmonica player, who one of my field assistants discovered playing at the Club Tavern in Middleton.

Andy later said that by 1998, he didn't get nervous before performances, but earlier he had been nervous playing with us. Really nervous.
He'd never played with anything approaching a band as big as ours. He
said he was even nervous before our rehearsal at the Humanities Building, but the band gave him such a warm welcome that it made things
easier. I liked hearing that.

Andy said that out there on the tiny stage at the end of the long catwalk at the Kohl Center he struggled to find a sweet spot where he could
hear the band and also hear himself at a good mix level. He found the
sweet spot, all right. Andy played two Jazz Crusaders tunes, and a faster
number, receiving a rousing standing ovation when he was finished. It
was an interesting dynamic: Andy is self-taught, doesn't read music,
and of course the band was reading. Most of what Andy does is impro-
visational, and he had to cue me when he was finished. But it worked—
it really worked. The band sensed this guy was something special and
took it up a notch, which further inspired Andy. To this day if you ask
him about his most memorable shows, that performance tops the list.

I haven't watched that first Kohl Center show recently—I could,
Wisconsin Public Television began taping and broadcasting the performances—but my guess is that I was fairly animated while conducting
the band. My feeling on conducting is that I try to be versatile and let
the music dictate my presentation. If it's a dramatic piece, I'll be a bit
more flamboyant. If it's something by Wagner, I'll be more straightforward. The problem with my approach is that people can't easily label
what kind of conductor I am. People think if I'm flamboyant I can't be
serious about the music. But when I do calm down, the reaction I get
is What's wrong? It's a quandary, but remember, you are reading this
analysis from a guy who used to climb a ladder, put his hat on backward, and flap his arms like a chicken, just like the Fifth Quarter crowd
doing the chicken dance.

More seriously, while conducting on football Saturdays at Camp Randall, I took the responsibility for setting the tempo. Many band directors would prefer the drum major do that. My philosophy was I set the tempo because I had written the arrangements and I knew what the tempos were supposed to be. If a drum major fouls up a tempo, he really feels lousy. If I foul it up, it's on me, and that's OK. It took some pressure off them. I liked conducting. I'll admit, unashamedly, that I came alive with the music. I don't think I was overly flamboyant. I tried to give the audience—and the band—what the music dictated. If you're placid and stoic, the musicians are not going to respond. It's what Ray Dvorak said, as explained earlier in this narrative: it's not the hand, it's the emotion. And you have to convey that emotion somehow.

Speaking of the hand, I never used a baton at the spring concerts. I honestly thought it was a little pretentious. I treated the varsity band more like a big jazz ensemble, and you don't see guys using a baton with a jazz ensemble. I did use a baton on the football field, partly because I felt it gave me more extension so people could see. But I don't like batons that are too long. I like hollow cane batons as opposed to plastic ones, though they're hard to find. I want a pear-shaped cork handle. One baton isn't necessarily better than another—what matters is what you like and are accustomed to using.

In summer 1998 the band was invited to participate in what was billed as a "Wisconsin tailgate party" as part of the Smithsonian Institution's Folklife Festival in Washington, DC. It was Wisconsin's sesquicentennial, and the state's display was the featured attraction, along with displays from the Philippines, the Baltic nations, and the Rio Grande. We were invited somewhat at the last minute, out of the blue, but it turned out to be a terrific trip. Many of the band members hadn't been to DC. We were able to fit in quite a bit of sightseeing. We saw some of the Smithsonian museums—they opened the Holocaust Museum during off-hours so we could get a tour—and all the major monuments.

We played on a makeshift football field set up on the National Mall. It was an all-star tailgate party the evening of July 3. Governor Tommy Thompson spoke, shouting, "Who can party better than somebody from Wisconsin?" Packers' announcer Jim Irwin was the MC. We played "Varsity," "You've Said It All," and a special version of "Stars and Stripes Forever"—half the band played the familiar Sousa march while the other half played "On, Wisconsin!"

The '98 football Badgers got off to a terrific start, winning their first nine games. It set them up for a chance to secure a Rose Bowl bid with a win on November 14 at Michigan. As it happened, the band was scheduled to make the trip to Ann Arbor. During the week, one of the Badgers' assistant coaches told one of my assistants, "We're glad you chose this one, because it's such a big game."

I wish we could have claimed to have planned it that way. The back-story is that while we tried to get to one Big Ten road football game each year, it was never guaranteed, and we couldn't cherry-pick the one we wanted. Quite a bit entered into it. Every spring I would write a letter to the athletic director of all the schools the football Badgers would visit in the fall (copying the school's band director), and generally say we were interested in taking the band to their stadium, and was there any reason why that would be problematic?

For a time there was a rule—I was never sure whether it was written or unwritten—that you couldn't take a visiting band to a school's home-coming Saturday.

In any case, I'd write those letters in the spring and wait for the responses. You might be surprised at how few places really wanted us to come. Some years, only one school said it was OK. There were numerous times that Iowa made it abundantly clear that they didn't want us to come—although we did go there on a couple of occasions. Often the excuse was they wouldn't have seating for us. I never bought that—I was writing six months in advance.

It was always special to go to Ohio State or Michigan—the big stadiums, the raucous crowds. Our trip to Ann Arbor in 1998 was our first there in a decade. Alas, the Badgers lost, 27–10. Because of the tie-breaking system that was in place at the time, the Badgers could still get to Pasadena by beating Penn State at Camp Randall the following Saturday. (If teams had identical win-loss records, the school that had gone the longest without a Rose Bowl appearance got to go. Michigan and Ohio State had both been to Pasadena since the Badgers went in 1994.)

Wisconsin beat Penn State, 24–3, to earn a return trip to Pasadena. It was exciting, though the stadium security had talked to me about the possibility of the fans rushing the field after a victory, or during our Fifth Quarter performance. They asked that I be ready to shut it down if that happened. Fortunately, it didn't.

The day was special for me in another way. At halftime, the entire band formed the number 30 on the field as a way to honor my thirty years as director. It was something they did on numerous significant anniversaries, and I always appreciated it. It required the band to get to Saturday morning practice early—before sunrise—to rehearse it, then leave and come back for our scheduled rehearsal. Sometimes my field assistants would take me out for an anniversary breakfast to be sure I wouldn't see the early practice. On the day of the Penn State game, they also presented Phyllis with thirty roses.

The band had a great time at the 1999 Rose Bowl but, to be honest, none of the subsequent Pasadena trips approached the wide-eyed wonder that accompanied us through the whole week five years earlier. In 1994, it had been *three decades* since Wisconsin had played in Pasadena. Many doubted we ever would again. As I've noted, there was red everywhere that week, endless celebrations, every day better than the day before. There was just no way to repeat that feeling five years later.

That said, we still had great fun. We performed again at Disneyland, and our performance drew excellent reviews. Jim Christensen and his wife, Karen, came, and I spent some time with them. Jim had been director of the marching band at UW–Madison and left to be music director at Disneyland before I arrived. We knew each other and made a point of getting together when the band went to California. But I almost missed the start of our '99 Rose Bowl Disney show. I'd been to a meeting on game day logistics and then got stuck in traffic on the Santa Ana Freeway. A Madison newspaper mentioned this episode, noting in a memorable phrase that I made it on time after being "rescued from the Pinocchio Parking Lot by Disney Security." From that point on, I sent a substitute to meetings that were scheduled in front of one of our performances. L.A. traffic can go sideways in a hurry.

The '99 game itself was tremendous, with the Badgers pulling off a 38–31 win over UCLA—ranked sixth in the country—behind a great rushing performance by Ron Dayne. The victory was particularly sweet because critics had been knocking the Big Ten selection system and saying Ohio State should have been in Pasadena.

Before the game, the analyst Craig James inanely went so far as to say the Badgers were "the worst team to ever play in the Rose Bowl." After dispatching the Bruins, Barry Alvarez had a wry retort. "Well," he said, "I know we're at least the second worst."

nine

RIDING HIGH

In March 1999, a front-page headline in the *Capital Times* read "UW Band Stands Up Kids."

About two thousand Madison-area schoolchildren showed up one morning at the Madison Civic Center expecting a performance from the marching band. We weren't there. It was embarrassing, I felt terrible, and we did a makeup show. How did it happen? The date had been changed at least once, and we just weren't in sync on the schedule with the Civic Center.

What that unfortunate episode really spotlighted was how overwhelming the demands on the band had become. Scheduling requests were a real problem. It seemed like groups were at us constantly—can you do this, can you do that?

I remembered back almost thirty years when the men's hockey coach Bob Johnson had hectored me into taking a part of the varsity band to hockey games after seeing us at the Field House for basketball. Three decades later, we'd played at virtually every sport. Maybe we missed fencing—but that was discontinued in the early 1990s.

A group of the varsity band played on a barge in the middle of Lake Wingra for the crew team. We played on the first tee before the opening drives at a golf match. We did track, soccer, wrestling, and more.

We played at a UW men's swim meet—well, we tried. The band practiced right across the street from the university's pool in the Natatorium. Jack Pettinger, the men's swim coach, was always asking me to take the band to a meet. I liked Jack. He was a fun guy who began his coaching career at Indiana University under the legendary James "Doc" Counsilman. Jack came to UW as head swim coach in 1969, the same year I arrived as band director.

Jack kept after me about playing, so one day when I knew there was a swim meet I told about twenty members of the band to meet me at the Natatorium.

"We're going to go up into the balcony and play."

We climbed up there and set up to perform. I looked down and saw Jack standing by the edge of the pool. We started to play, and suddenly Jack turned, faced up toward us, and began waving his arms frantically over his head. He was signaling for us to stop. It turned out the Natatorium echoed worse than Mammoth Cave. We stopped immediately—though I still count that as a performance.

At one point, we became so inundated with requests for the band that I decided to basically say no to everything beyond football, basketball, hockey, and our spring concert.

The kids weren't happy, but I told them I just didn't have the time or inclination to organize what was becoming a complex behemoth. They came back at me with an idea. "What if one of us takes over the organizing?"

I said I'd try it for a while. And it worked. They took responsibility. There were a few hiccups, but all in all, it was a success. I put some rules in place. They couldn't schedule anything opposite men's basketball or hockey. And they had to have a minimum number of players—fifteen band members—committed or they would have to call off the appearance.

Be careful what you wish for: the band's soaring popularity is what I'd wanted to see happen from the outset. Given my personality, it's easy to get overenthusiastic. It happened at our first varsity band concert in April 1999, when we were celebrating the twenty-fifth anniversary of the spring concerts. It wasn't a bad show by any means, but I was so intent on celebrating twenty-five years and making a big splash that I kept adding things. A record Thursday crowd of more than sixty-five hundred showed up. The concert, including an intermission, lasted three hours and fifteen minutes, which is too long. There is an old show business expression about leaving the audience wanting more, and I didn't do it on that Thursday. It was a valuable lesson for me. We shortened the show considerably the next two nights.

~

The Badgers earned a return Rose Bowl engagement that fall, and it was interesting for us because, at least in some quarters, the competition between the marching bands received nearly as much attention as the football teams.

It was Wisconsin versus Stanford, and to some observers that meant that two untraditional marching bands known for pushing the envelope of propriety would be performing in Pasadena. I took considerable exception to that view. The Stanford band—"almost completely student run," to quote a Madison newspaper story during Rose Bowl week—was notorious for shows that had sexual innuendo, which we would never do. There was more, tending to the silly and sarcastic. That fall they had all worn handicapped parking signs during a game against UCLA, after a scandal in which Bruin football players were caught using handicapped parking permits. The Stanford band's most infamous moment came near the end of a 1982 game against UC Berkeley, when the band stormed the field before the final whistle, inadvertently blocking several members of the Stanford kickoff team and helping Cal score a winning, game-ending touchdown.

That wasn't us—hardly. I frankly became tired of all the comparisons and at one point during the week gave a television interview in which I said, "They need to do what they need to do. The big difference between the bands is, when we want to be good, we can be."

I regretted that remark as soon as it came out of my mouth, but it was true. They never were serious. It was all fun for them.

I regretted it a little less after reading a quote in a newspaper that week from a Stanford band member who used Stanford's exacting academic standards to excuse their excesses.

"Everybody at Stanford works really, really hard in terms of academics," he said. "It would be terrible to come to practice and have someone barking at you all the time when you have so many other pressures. We don't have 10 hours a week to spend on precision marching where a normal band might because of our academic concerns."

Talk about pretentious! You can bet nobody had eaten a rock in Palo Alto.

The day of the game, we played a Beach Boys show that was very well received. Stanford's performance was—let me be diplomatic—unexceptional. There was no interaction or animosity between the bands on game day. I think the people who anticipated there might be were disappointed.

Six weeks after that 2000 Rose Bowl—which the Badgers won, besting Stanford 17–9—I took 150 members of the band to Green Bay, where we made our first appearance at the city's wonderful hall, the Weidner Center for the Performing Arts. Great artists and shows had shone at the Weidner since its 1993 opening, including Tony Bennett, Harry Belafonte, and Willie Nelson, and the musicals *The Phantom of the Opera* and *Miss Saigon*.

The Weidner was a major venue for us to play, and they treated us like we were a major act. I think our high profile from the Rose Bowl appearances as well as having played during Packers games at Lambeau led to the invitation. There was also a considerable UW alumni contingent living in the area. We gave two performances on Saturday, February 19, and sold out the 1,850 seats each time, raising more than $23,000 for UW scholarships for Green Bay–area students.

We continued to play the Weidner annually while I was band director. We did take it down to one show after two or three years out of concern for the band's time and stamina.

That first year, we played a medley from *Miss Saigon*, an operatic musical that I like a lot. The next day the *Green Bay Press-Gazette* reviewer mentioned that the entire musical *Miss Saigon*, and others, had played the Weidner, though "none sparked as much sheer spirit as the UW Band."

The reviewer also noted that at one point the tuba section directed a question at the Green Bay audience:

"What's the difference between Mike Leckrone and Lambeau Field?"

The answer: "One's old and needs renovating and the other one's a stadium."

Those tuba section skyrockets were generally a big hit, though there came a point when—as college kids will do—they began pushing the envelope of propriety. I told them they were going to have to run them by me—or one of my assistants—before using them at a performance. It didn't really cramp their style. It made them more creative.

～

One thing I said from the Weidner stage—"It's a great time to be a Badger"—continued to reverberate through 2000. In April, Dick Bennett's men's basketball team did what many considered the impossible and made it to the NCAA Final Four in Indianapolis. We were invited to go, unlike the time the hockey team first made it, in the early 1970s, to what became the Frozen Four. From the beginning, the NCAA saw the value of having bands as part of the Final Four basketball atmosphere. We were welcomed and never saw a hotel bill.

The thing about the Final Four in basketball—we'd eventually get to two more during my time—was that, unlike the Rose Bowl week, it all happens so fast. It's difficult to really savor it—to bank those moments of happiness.

The Badgers dropped their semifinal game in Indianapolis against Michigan State, but that weekend topped a terrific sixteen-month run for UW athletics—and the band: two Rose Bowl appearances, the men's Final Four in basketball, a WCHA conference title in men's hockey, and an NIT championship in women's basketball. The last was accomplished before more than thirteen thousand fans at the Kohl Center when the Badgers defeated Florida 75–74.

It was an amazing sixteen months, and the band played at another football bowl game before 2000 was over, the Wells Fargo Sun Bowl in El Paso on December 29, which the Badgers won, 21–20, over UCLA.

One of our most memorable bowl experiences came two years later at the Alamo Bowl, December 28, 2002, in San Antonio. It was not memorable for the best of reasons, although we did get to play right outside the Alamo. They wouldn't let us play inside, which we understood.

But what anyone associated with the band remembers about the Alamo Bowl is a severe flu outbreak that nearly decimated us.

It seemed every time I came to rehearsal, I'd hear that another six or seven musicians were down with the flu. It came very close to us having to march with a blank spot or two, though I don't think that happened. I told the band I felt like General Custer. Every time I turned around, another kid was dropping. I remember vividly that when we finished the half-time show, two of the players ran off the field and were sick to their stomachs.

Flying home was particularly treacherous. On the way from the hotel to the airport, the bus stopped at a convenience store, and one of my assistants, Janice Stone, went in and bought a bunch of plastic garbage bags and passed them around in case anyone got sick on the plane. I'm sure people did. It was a tough trip. At least the game itself was memorable for the right reason: the Badgers beat Colorado in a thriller, 31–28, in overtime.

As for the spring concerts, we were getting accustomed to and enjoying the Kohl Center as a venue. I should shout-out Rod MacDonald, who worked at both the Kohl Center and Monona Terrace and was at the ready whenever I needed a set built or some piece of equipment for a prop. Rod also had a great eye for production.

We called our 2001 spring concert "2001: A Band Odyssey," and we worked in numerous references to the famous 1968 Stanley Kubrick *2001: A Space Odyssey* movie that inspired our show. We had been playing the theme song since the mid-1980s. It's actually a piece by Richard

Strauss titled *Also Sprach Zarathustra*. We'd used it in some shows that included classical music, along with another that became a favorite, Tchaikovsky's *1812 Overture* with "On, Wisconsin!" tucked inside.

With "2001," we'd been playing it straight, and then at some point our drummers began adding the drum beat that is now so recognizable. I liked it right away and there was an immediate audience reaction, people clapping along. I simplified the horns' part a little bit, but as noted, the drum beat was spontaneous—some of my best ideas are other people's! We eventually added what we called "Space Badgers" to the Fifth Quarter—we were always looking for ways to make sure those postgame performances weren't the same old, same old.

That spring 2001 show marked a return of Tom Wopat, who had helped us close out our Field House performances in 1997 and was always welcome. Less welcome—at least in our 2001 skits—was the Kubrick movie's sinister computer, HAL 9000, which kept popping up and bedeviling me throughout the show. At one point I facetiously noted it had clearly been created at the University of Illinois.

After so many years—the 2001 spring concert was our twenty-seventh—I was gratified to read the following in Rob Thomas's review of the concert in the *Capital Times*: "This year's event was another stellar evening, once again striking that satisfying balance between a big band concert and a pep rally."

Two months later, in June 2001, I was asked to give the commencement address at Monona Grove High School. I began with a preview of what I intended to tell my freshman class of band members at UW in a couple of months.

"I will tell them there is no such thing as happiness," I said.

I continued: "That is a terrible thing for a commencement speaker to say. But what I tell them is if you're expecting complete happiness, you're going to be disappointed. What you're going to experience in your life—whether it's a new job, a new school, or new friends—you'll experience moments of happiness. Dwell on those moments of happiness because there are going to be other times when you have to handle failure."

Later on, I told the students they should "be serious about what you do, but don't take yourself too seriously."

Which was easy to say for someone who regularly performed the chicken dance.

I liked what Principal Georgiana Giese said that day, too, at the conclusion, after presenting the class of 2001: "Please, remember to phone home."

I enjoyed that day at Monona Grove more than some of the UW commencements, when the band played and I conducted. Those were tough because we were asked to play the entire time graduates were receiving their diplomas, sometimes thirty minutes of continuous playing. It was a grind for the band kids.

I'd been asked to conduct at commencement by Chancellor Irving Shain after an episode in 1982 when former US Defense Secretary Melvin Laird was given an honorary degree during the ceremony. Laird had served as secretary during the Vietnam War, and awarding him this degree was highly controversial on campus. There were demonstrators outside Camp Randall and boos inside when Laird received his honorary doctor of laws degree.

A conductor from the School of Music handled the music program that day and chose to play a movement from *The Planets* by Gustav Holst.

It was titled "Mars, the Bringer of War."

Chancellor Shain sought me out and said, "From now on, you're doing commencement."

When our 2002 spring concerts were approaching, American Family Insurance reached out to me and suggested they sponsor a Mike Leckrone bobblehead doll that could be given away to lucky ticketholders to spur attendance on Thursday night. It worked. We drew nearly seven thousand people, our largest Thursday audience to date. One thousand of the bobbleheads were produced, and when concert goers entered the Kohl Center they were given a slip of colored paper with a song title on it. If that song was played during the second half of the show, they could turn in the paper for a free bobblehead. (The song was "Stars and Stripes Forever.") Others could purchase the bobbleheads for eight dollars.

There were more Mike Leckrone bobbleheads over the years, something I never pursued but also never minded. In 2016, members of the band who were traveling for spring break decided to take my bobblehead along and then post photos on social media. Some three hundred band members participated, and my bobblehead could be seen from Costa Rica to Niagara Falls. Channel 3 in Madison even did a feature on it, interviewing trombone player Kayla Huemer about what the kids were calling "Where in the world is Mike Leckrone?" Mark Koehn and Susan Siman asked Kayla what I thought about it all, and Kayla said, "He doesn't really like the limelight."

I imagine there were a few disbelieving guffaws across Madison when that was heard.

In 2019, the National Bobblehead Hall of Fame and Museum in Milwaukee released the final Mike Leckrone bobblehead, in honor of my retirement. It produced 2,019 of the dolls, which portrayed me in white pants and a red suit jacket, rings on my pinkies, standing on a base shaped like the band's logo. As a bonus, the bobblehead played "On, Wisconsin!"

The 2002 spring concert where the first bobblehead was introduced included trumpet player Stan Mark as a guest artist. Stan was a big-band guy who most famously played with Maynard Ferguson's band, which had a big hit with "Gonna Fly Now," the theme from the movie *Rocky*. Stan was gracious throughout our time together. We worked the *Rocky* theme into his performance, and he also did a fine tribute to trumpet virtuoso Conrad Gozzo. Another highlight of that show was a piano solo by our assistant drum major, Dan Henkel, during Gershwin's *Rhapsody in Blue*, which was likely the most ambitious piece we'd attempted in a spring show to that point. Dan did a great job, not surprising, as just two weeks later he performed a Gershwin tribute concert in Morphy Hall.

~

In late 2002 I was asked, and readily agreed, to serve on the honorary council of a new venture called the Wisconsin Center for Music Education. Other council members included Tom Wopat and former Wisconsin governor Lee Dreyfus.

The center, which would be first of its kind in the state if not the nation, was the brainchild of Mike George and Dick Wolf, retired music educators who had been members of the marching band at UW. Dick later served as an assistant with the band for many years.

They'd begun fundraising in 2001, in the wake of the 9/11 attacks—a difficult economy. Raising the money took some time. But the center opened in 2005, in a new building in Waunakee, a grand opening that also included a fundraising silent auction of guitars autographed by Les Paul, George Benson, Peter Frampton, Aerosmith's Joe Perry, and several others.

The center houses the Wisconsin Foundation of School Music, the Wisconsin School Music Association, and the Wisconsin Music Educators Association. I was extremely honored in 2007 to receive the second-ever Lifetime Achievement Award from the Wisconsin Foundation of School Music. The first, awarded in 2004, went to Waukesha native Les Paul, long recognized as one of the great guitarists of his generation and creator of a solid body of electric guitar music that, in the words of his award citation, "paved the way for rock and roll." It was one of many of Paul's recording innovations.

I received my award at a ceremony on November 14, 2007, a festive evening that included performances by our band's drum line, along with the alumni band and Very Special Arts Wisconsin choir. Music educators (and gifted musicians) Grant Manhart and Frank Tracz spoke, as did Pat Richter, Tom Wopat, and Elizabeth Burmaster, state superintendent of public instruction. Of the accomplishments that were mentioned in the program as contributing to my receiving the award, I particularly liked this one: "He brings the 'wow factor' to music education."

There have been two more recipients of the Lifetime Achievement Award in the years since: Marvin Rabin (2011), founder of the Wisconsin

Youth Symphony Orchestra and a longtime music educator; and Milwaukee native Al Jarreau (2016), a legendary performer and winner of
seven Grammy Awards.

I'm honored to be in their company. The Wisconsin Center for
Music Education is where my extensive collection of music recordings
and books will reside when I'm gone.

～

One interesting thing about serving as marching band director for as
long as I did is that it can put a historical lens on problems or controversies that are bubbling in the moment. This happened at the start of
the 2003 football season. The Badgers hosted Akron at Camp Randall—
and won the game 48–31—but one of the most prominent news stories
in the game's aftermath involved the decision not to play "Jump Around,"
the song by House of Pain that had delighted the Camp Randall crowd
and especially the students since it was first played in 1998.

The song played over the public address during the break between
the third and fourth quarters. I was never upset that it wasn't the band
playing it. It had everyone jumping up and down, and I was all for anything that got the stadium going. Our band members jumped around
as much as anybody. I enjoyed watching the spectacle. Sometimes even
the opposing team would be jumping around on the sideline. That was
interesting.

The perceived problem was that the people jumping up and down in
the stadium's upper deck were causing it to sway, which perhaps understandably made some people nervous. Athletic director Pat Richter
made the decision not to play "Jump Around" between the third and
fourth quarters of the Akron game. News stories in the days that followed
quoted outraged students and others criticizing Richter for dumping a
cherished Camp Randall tradition.

I was able to note—when a reporter asked—that this was not the
first swaying-upper-deck squabble at Camp Randall. Some twenty-five
years earlier—in the middle of the 1978 football season—then athletic
director Elroy Hirsch asked me not to play "You've Said It All" until at

least ten minutes after the game had ended. As happened in 2003, there had been complaints that the dancing and jumping that accompanied our playing the beloved polka was causing the upper deck to shake.

Elroy told me the UW Planning and Construction Department and State Bureau of Facilities Management were calling in an engineering consultant, the Madison firm Arnold and O'Sheridan, to determine the structural safety of the upper deck. In the meantime, we had to abide by the ten-minutes-after-the-game rule.

Budweiser, of course, used the song in its advertising. Once the upper deck controversy surfaced, Budweiser—unlikely to ever pass up a chance for publicity—gave us promotional wristwatches to toss into the stands after the game when it was finally time for us to play "You've Said It All."

The safety study was completed in time for the home opener in September 1979. According to Elroy, it showed that the swaying was no threat and that the upper deck could support a crowd three times larger than its approximate thirteen-thousand-seat capacity.

The "Jump Around" controversy in 2003 was settled much more quickly. The safety review took only a matter of days, and Chancellor John Wiley told the *Wisconsin State Journal* that "Jump Around" would be back for the second home game.

The motion of the upper deck, Wiley said, "is actually very, very small, and far below any risk to the integrity of the deck." He did ask the upper deck patrons to consider simply cheering on the students below rather than jumping themselves.

$\sim$

The next month, October 2003, brought an old friend to Madison. Bob Reynolds, the man who hired me to come to Wisconsin in 1969, accompanied the Detroit Chamber Winds, an ensemble made up of members of the Detroit Symphony, for a concert at Mills Hall. Bob was the conductor. We made a point of getting together. Some people were surprised that Bob and I got along so well. We did have different personalities. Bob was straightforward, very proper, and I—well, let's just say it would be hard to imagine Bob alongside me doing the chicken dance. I was the marching band guy, and he was the symphony guy—it wasn't automatic that we would hit it off. But we respected each other, and, as with a lot of things, if you scratch the surface, you might find out you have similar interests underneath. Bob and I, for instance, shared an interest in jazz. We didn't see each other often but took advantage of it when we did.

The football team earned a bowl bid at the end of the 2003 season, an invitation to face Auburn in the Music City Bowl in Nashville. The band was invited, too, except it wasn't the invitation we might have hoped for. It was a relatively new bowl game, and perhaps the organizers didn't realize how passionate fans—especially Wisconsin fans—are about their band. When we received the invitation in early December—the game was December 31—we were told the half-time ceremony would not involve the bands and instead would recognize Nashville-area youth sports.

I wasn't happy, and thought it ironic that a bowl named for music would preclude music at its half-time showcase. But once the media picked up the story, our fans unleashed "a torrent of angry correspondence," according to a story in the *Capital Times*. To their credit, the organizers regrouped and put forth a plan that had the designated home team—Auburn—sharing halftime with the youth sports recognition. Meanwhile, our band would play our traditional half-time show before the game and then give a Fifth Quarter performance immediately after the postgame trophy presentation.

I thought it an adequate compromise, and I issued a written statement asking our fans to please tone down their vitriol: "Though I appreciate how passionately the community supports the band, our fans' reaction is becoming a distraction for band members and those who are working hard to make the game a great experience for all fans. The performance schedule is fair to both bands and gives ample opportunity to see us perform."

We also joined Auburn in a "battle of the bands" the night before the game at the Wildhorse Saloon on Second Street in downtown Nashville. We fared better in that contest than the football Badgers did the next day, when they lost to the Tigers, 28–14.

~

The following April marked the thirtieth annual varsity band concert. Rhythm, the combined entertainment section of the *Capital Times* and *Wisconsin State Journal*, printed an interview with me that was mostly about the history of the spring shows but also included the following question:

"Any consideration that you've done it all?"

My answer: "You're being tactful asking about my future. I don't have any immediate or long-range plans. I often quote Duke Ellington, who was asked a lot in his later years about when he would retire, and he said, 'To do what?' I feel the same way."

The truth is, I'd been asked about the possibility of retiring ever since our trip to the 1994 Rose Bowl. I'd been at the University of Wisconsin for twenty-five years at that point. People would ask, "How much longer do you see yourself doing this?" Some people suggested that there was no way I was going to be able to top that Rose Bowl experience. On one hand, they were right. There was no topping it. But I was nowhere near ready to retire in 1994.

Then I guess I got stubborn. In simple terms, I loved what I was doing. Why would I stop? I was having too much fun to stop. There were bureaucratic responsibilities that came with being a professor, but over time I was able to siphon many of those out of my day-to-day routine. Faculty meetings, for instance. I often had an event to go to that conflicted with meetings, in which case I missed the meetings. It was the truth—I *did* have events to go to—but it was also a convenient out.

The only time I ever really considered retirement, and then only for a dark evening or two, came a few years later, at the nadir of a situation involving the behavior of some members of the band.

But that's getting ahead of the story.

ten

MILESTONES AND MISSTEPS

A career highlight occurred in September 2004 when our varsity band was invited to play during the opening weekend of Madison's Overture Center for the Arts, a state-of-the-art venue just off the Capitol Square that was gifted to the city by philanthropists Pleasant Rowland and her husband, Jerry Frautschi.

Overture contains multiple performance spaces and galleries and was something that Madison, frankly, had needed for a long time. The acoustics in the main theater, Overture Hall, are terrific. And that's where we were invited to play at noon on Sunday, September 19—the first group to play Overture Hall.

The night before, the hall featured performances by André De Shields, Ethan Stiefel, Tracy Nelson, and Ben Sidran. Sunday night, the Madison Symphony would play.

We were honored to kick things off Sunday afternoon. I told the band it was a big deal, saying that one day they might well come to Overture with their kids and be able to say they were part of the opening ceremony.

I like to think our invitation came in part because Overture—wisely, in my opinion—wanted to dispel any notion that it wouldn't be a fun place to go. There was room for the symphony *and* the chicken dance. We surely tested the new acoustics that first afternoon with a program that included rock and roll, Broadway show tunes, jazz, and a tribute to Ray Charles.

Early, I called out to the crowd, "This may be the Overture Center, but this is the UW Varsity Band, and we're going to play that 'Hey!' song."

And we did.

In the years that followed, we performed numerous times at Overture, including a series of children's concerts. I would get a call in late summer, once they'd set their schedule of Broadway shows and so forth. They would suggest dates—often they were Thursdays and Fridays—and bus in kids from area schools to see us.

We enjoyed doing it. Those young students were a great audience—they really didn't care what you sounded like, and they were enthusiastic, which the band always appreciates. I would generally begin by calling out: "Where you all from?" Naturally, the students from different schools would try to out-shout each other. It broke the ice.

I asked Overture to slate the shows in the morning, which was better for the band members' schedules, and there was a Thursday morning a year or so after the Overture opening that was particularly memorable.

A few months earlier I'd received a call from St. James School in Madison. A part-time music teacher there, Shirley Robinson, would be attending one of the Overture children's shows in early February 2006 as part of the St. James contingent.

The person who called told me that Shirley, then seventy-three years young, was a UW–Madison alumnus who in the 1950s had hoped to play in the UW Marching Band, only to learn that it was male only. Shirley went on to a distinguished music teaching career in Prairie du Sac, Madison, and Monona, and after "retiring" accepted the half-time position at St. James.

On the day the St. James crew attended, I surprised Shirley by asking her to leave her seat and come onstage. I explained to the audience that fifty years earlier, as a UW student, she'd played with the concert band—one of only eight women—but now at Overture she was playing tambourine with the UW Varsity Band. The crowd loved it and so did she.

$\sim$

There was some history, too, in our acquiring nineteen new drums in fall 2004. Two decades earlier, a member of our marching band, Dan Getzen, witnessed his father making a substantial donation of trumpets to the band. By 2004, Dan was working for D.E.G. Music Products in the Lake Geneva area and helped broker a deal that brought us a line of Dynasty drums: nine snares, four trios, three twenty-four-inch bass, and three twenty-eight-inch bass.

We liked not only Dan's earlier connection to the band but the fact that D.E.G. was nearby, so it would not be difficult to get replacement parts. Drums, being played constantly, wear out quickly. The only snag was that Dan had some difficulty finding the bright silver color I wanted to match our other silver instruments. The laminate they were using wasn't bright enough. But Dan called around and found one that worked.

In January 2005, I had fun emceeing what was called a Community of Stars Concert at the Middleton Performing Arts Center. The stars included friends like Kitt Reuter-Foss, "Westside Andy" Linderman, Leotha Stanley, Kelly DeHaven, and Ginny O'Brien—along with a percussionist who was more than a friend, my son Erik Leckrone.

Erik was interested in music from a very young age. He played percussion in the Middleton High School band and as a member of the school's jazz ensemble, having taken lessons from Vicki Jenks and with Pat Greenan at Ward-Brodt. His undergraduate degree was in music performance–percussion from Northern Illinois University—and then he attended California State University, Long Beach, for graduate school.

Erik worked and played in Southern California for several years but eventually moved to the Nashville area. The California traffic wore him down. He called once and said he felt like he was spending more time driving to and from gigs than actually playing them. He also felt there might be more opportunities in Nashville for a working musician. He's not a headline player—I don't know that he wants to be—but he's very good and a solid professional.

Erik can play any percussion: a drum set, a mallet, or timpani. He can do it all. He's a wonderful sight reader—playing something new just by reading it off a page. He's a consummate professional, a team player who learned early there's little upside for a musician in challenging a director, even when you disagree. Erik also teaches percussion at Motlow State Community College south of Nashville.

All of my kids enjoy music. My son Kris played tuba in the marching band. Two of my daughters played clarinet, not in the marching band but the concert groups. My third daughter was active in choral groups. I think music was important to them, and it's something that stays with you forever. I told my kids what I try to tell everyone: you don't have to be a professional to have music in your life.

One of the more intriguing professional musicians to cross my path in Madison knocked on my office door in the Humanities Building one day early in 2006. His name was Sergei Belkin, and he was a native of Ukraine. His knock was shy, if that's possible. Sergei was extraordinarily bashful. One of my assistants had seen him play accordion at a festival outside Madison and insisted that we meet.

"He's phenomenal," my assistant said.

But I'd learned that sometimes people get swept up in the musical atmosphere of the moment and what they recall as phenomenal really isn't.

When I opened the office door, Sergei quietly said, "I play accordion, and I was told you might be interested."

"Well," I said, "I need to hear you play."

"Right now?" he said.

Sergei was then thirty-three years old. I learned later that at age three he lost his father to a motorcycle accident. His grandparents bought him a toy accordion. Within a few years he'd exchanged it for the real thing and proved gifted enough that he was accepted at the Moscow Conservatory, where Tchaikovsky taught in the 1800s.

After a series of moves, Sergei ended up in Madison, determined to earn a living with his accordion, no easy task. I was to discover there was a showman lurking behind the shy exterior. When Sergei came into my office that day and played, he was really good. He had great keyboard technique. He was transformed when he picked up the accordion. I invited him to play at our varsity band concerts in April 2006.

Sergei played two numbers at the concerts and completely charmed the crowd, which gave him a standing ovation. They caught his personality. He was a huge hit. One night as he walked to the Kohl Center stage, someone tossed him a cowboy hat and he jauntily slapped it on.

Sergei Belkin stayed in Madison. The last I heard of him was July 2019—pre-pandemic—when he was the featured player with the Wisconsin Chamber Orchestra on a program that concluded with *Finlandia*, the best-known work of Jean Sibelius, a composer I greatly admire.

I might note that it was not unusual for someone to play for me in my office. Every August, in combination with the on-the-field band tryouts, I would audition students in my office. I wanted to hear everyone play. I tried to do the office auditions first.

I had a schedule for the office auditions, bringing the kids in at about eight-minute intervals. Later, when more and more kids wanted to be in the band, I trimmed it to six minutes. I'd often begin by asking, "How good are you?" It was interesting: Most of those who were really good downplayed it, while the ones who weren't very good exaggerated their ability. Of course, there were a few who were good and didn't hesitate to tout it. I'm afraid I may have been a little like that when I auditioned for my scholarship at Butler.

In the early days I had people show up who couldn't play at all. They thought it was a way to see all the football games. When we started, as many as one in five who tried out really weren't qualified. Later, when word circulated about what was required, that we'd established a standard, far fewer unqualified kids showed up—maybe one in twenty.

In those first auditions, along with making sure they could play, I wanted to try to ascertain a work ethic. Did they have a desire to be successful? The playing itself was easier to quantify. I didn't have to hear much to know if they knew what they were doing. They could bring in a piece they wanted to play, but I also always had them sight-read something. Give me thirty seconds, and I could tell if they were band material or not. Now, ranking them against other players of similar ability—that would take much longer.

The month following our 2006 varsity band concert with Sergei Belkin, I was asked to participate in—of all things—a medical school graduation. As often happens when you just go with the flow, it turned out to be a lot of fun.

I received a call from Phil Farrell, dean of the UW School of Medicine, who said two of his pending May 2006 graduates were alumni of the marching band. Maybe we could have some fun with that?

David Gazeley played tuba and Anne Daul played trumpet in the band. They'd gone to high school in Green Bay and were with the band for two Rose Bowl trips. They were to be seated in the fourth row for the graduation ceremony at the Wisconsin Union Theater, and Dean Farrell planned to ask them to come up onstage and join a small current band ensemble that was playing at the event. David and Anne would protest that they didn't have instruments. At which point I would bound onstage, wearing my red blazer, and hand each of them an instrument.

That's pretty much what happened. They were good sports, took the instruments, and played. I think Dean Farrell got a bigger kick out of it than anyone. I was able to express my shock that a tuba player was actually graduating from medical school. David was headed for a residency in internal medicine at the Tufts Medical Center in Boston; Anne's residency was at the Carolinas Medical Center in Charlotte.

~

In August 2006, a *Wisconsin State Journal* reporter showed up to do a feature on band tryouts, and it gave me a chance to reflect on how far we'd come in that regard in my time in Madison. I was seventy that summer, in my thirty-eighth year as band director. I could think back to the start when we were practically pleading with kids to come out for the band; now we had too many and I had to turn people away. The numbers swelled after the 1994 Rose Bowl. Sometimes I had to say no to as many as 150 people. Of those, maybe fifty would be gone the first day of their own accord. They'd anticipated the fun part but not the work part.

I also was concerned about whether the high numbers would last. Each year I started designating a few kids who were close but not good enough at that point to get in.

I told them, "You're not going to march on the field this year, but you can come to rehearsals, see what's going on and learn the music, and then you can play in the varsity band the second semester, at basketball and hockey games." It helped when our numbers started to dip, which inevitably they did from the post–Rose Bowl peaks. But the decline wasn't significant. More than three hundred still came out.

The *State Journal* reporter noted that I made a point of trying to learn and remember the names of the freshmen. He wrote that I walked up to a trumpet player and said, "You're from West High School. Your last name starts with an *S*. Is it Shelley?"

"Schalley," the trumpet player said.

I was close. I didn't mention it to the reporter, but I started being purposeful about trying to learn everyone's name during my first year in Madison. Of course, the band was smaller then. But I felt, in 1969, that since I was the third band director in three years, everything probably seemed strange to the kids, and I wanted to try to create a bond. Make them feel less like just a face in the crowd. I purposely learned their names. Once you do it, that becomes an expectation. I had to make sure I knew people's names. I worked at it, probably harder than the kids realized.

I did two things that really helped. Any chance I had to write a kid's name down, I'd write it down. Not just say it—write it down. "What's your name again?" I'd say. I had all sorts of forms and pretended I needed their names more than once. The other thing was a tip someone gave me. When you're introduced to someone, make a point of saying their name out loud. Maybe pretend you didn't hear it quite right. "Was that John Doe? Oh, great, John Doe. Nice to meet you, John." That really did help me bank names and faces. One of the reasons I worked hard at it was that it carries more force—is much more intimidating—when someone up in the tower says, "Hey, Bill, get in step!" Rather than "Hey, you in the red shirt." They knew I knew their names. I think it helped them understand they were responsible to me and to each other and couldn't just go and hide. It was purposeful. I had a knack for it, which I've noticed has lapsed since I'm not doing it regularly.

I made a point of being in good physical shape myself by the time summer tryouts commenced. My preferred exercise was jumping rope, something I started back in high school in Indiana. Our basketball coach used it for conditioning. He also believed it could help prevent shin splints. I don't know if there is any truth to that, but in all the marching I did I never did get shin splints. In Madison I was given a jump rope by the man who called himself the Jump Rope King—Bobby Hinds, a colorful former Badger varsity boxing champion who ran a successful company that made jump ropes and lightweight rubber-tubing gym equipment.

Once I became band director, I would step up my jump-roping in early July, usually in the heat of the afternoons, so I'd be ready for the August tryouts.

～

The 2006 UW football season began with three nonconference victories at Camp Randall Stadium. Game four was the first conference matchup, on the road against Michigan. The band made the trip to Ann Arbor, and on one of the buses coming home to Madison—a 27–13 loss to the Wolverines—there was some rowdy behavior that in the minds of at least a few kids crossed a line of propriety. They subsequently complained to UW administrators.

It was not the first time in my nearly forty years as band director that the propriety envelope had been pushed, or even pushed past. Our mantra as a band insisted on the kids working extremely hard—eat a rock!—while allowing for fun too. Realistically, when your group consists of nearly three hundred college-age students, there are going to be occasions when lines get crossed. I had been on buses when it happened—the good-taste line, anyway. Nothing more serious than that. When something more serious did happen on a bus I wasn't on, I'd generally hear about it from band members who weren't involved—and were concerned about the band's reputation—at which point we would address it.

In 2004, I received a call saying a band bus coming home from the Big Ten women's basketball tournament in Indianapolis had stopped in Illinois—and alerted state police—because a belligerent band member was out of control. I was able to reach the bus driver on a cell phone and spoke with the individual causing the problem.

"That settled him right down," the bus driver later told a reporter.

It bothered me enough that I decided not to have the band play at the Big Ten men's tournament that followed. That drew everyone's attention, as it was supposed to. Then we did play at the first NCAA men's tournament game in Milwaukee a week later, and we were back on track.

On the bus home from Michigan in September 2006, the concern was hazing. I received a stern letter on October 3, ten days after the game, from Chancellor John Wiley, stating the band's culture had to change—or else. I remember saying to one of my assistants, "He thinks it's worse than it is." I felt we could deal with it—and would.

But at a meeting two days later, Wiley addressed the band in person. He was furious and said any band conduct that would not be tolerated in an academic classroom would bring serious consequences.

A few days later, on October 10, the gist of that meeting was reported in the Madison newspapers. The next day, a *Capital Times* editorial noted that no details of what happened on the Michigan bus had been released and asked: "Has Puritan Cotton Mather reappeared on campus in the form of Chancellor John Wiley?"

The *Cap Times* may have thought it was doing us a favor—the editorial was headlined "On the March against the Band"—but two days later Wiley's top assistant, Casey Nagy, held a press conference, releasing details of the bus trip and stating the administration's belief that sexual innuendo and hazing were too large a part of the band culture. I was at the press conference, too, and pointed out that the vast majority of band members knew the lines not to cross. "They have to learn to stand up," I said, "and say that's not acceptable for the Wisconsin band."

I was heartened when, on October 15, the *Capital Times* ran five letters to the editor about the episode, all in support of the band.

I will quote from one, sent by Dana DeGroot and family of Colby, Wisconsin, who wrote about their daughter's experience in the band:

> She was not a drinker, and was never made to feel uncomfortable for not drinking during social events. The band and staff provided her with a secure and loving family away from home, which nurtured her to become the confident UW graduate student she is today . . .
>
> As for the Michigan trip, we heard nothing but praise about the band from Michigan alumni and residents. During breakfast we sat next to Michigan alumni who thought the UW band was the best in the nation and that Mike Leckrone was a living legend. During the game we watched as the band professionally handled jeers and things being thrown at them by the Michigan student section. In turn, the band put on a tremendous performance.
>
> We would like to suggest that the chancellor interview more than just one or two disgruntled ex-band members, and perhaps speak to one of the over 300 band members, thousands of band alumni, and thousand[s] of supportive band parents and families before letting out caustic information to the media.

A year later, in September 2007, Casey Nagy told an Associated Press reporter that the administration was "very pleased" with the band's response. "We think the message was well received and behavior modified," Nagy said. "The band is back to being one of the great assets of the institution, which they should be."

Alas, we would be tested one more time, a year later, after another road trip to Ann Arbor, and another Badger loss, following three straight nonconference wins.

Michigan defeated the Badgers, 27–25, on September 27. It was late the following week that I first heard allegations about band behavior on the bus back home. It sounded dismayingly similar to what happened in 2006. I received word at 3:45 p.m. Friday, October 3, spoke briefly with the chancellor—a new one, Biddy Martin—and then I met with the band around 4:30. I told them I was suspending them—the entire band—from playing at the game the next night at Camp Randall against Ohio State.

Looking back, if I had to do it again, I would do it differently, which I'll explain momentarily. Nevertheless, I think the way I did handle it worked out for the best.

The band was stunned when I told them they were suspended. A *State Journal* reporter reached me by phone later that evening, and I told her they felt like I'd hit them between the eyes with a sledgehammer.

"You don't have any idea how hard it was," I told the reporter. "It's like I can remember my father saying, 'This is going to hurt me more than it hurts you.' They know how important this is to me."

I feel now that I shouldn't have suspended the whole band. I didn't have enough information at the time. I acted without proof, on hearsay, which I don't like to do. If the other episode two years earlier hadn't happened, I wouldn't have reacted as I did the second time. I would have gone more slowly, found those responsible, and suspended them. But I didn't. It was a traumatic period, and the one time in my fifty years at UW when I briefly considered walking away from the job.

I'm glad I didn't. I reinstated the band after the Ohio State game, and we found a path forward. We were given a liaison, Donna Freitag, with the dean of students office, and she was terrific. We created a mentorship program and an internal code of conduct. There were workshops on hazing and harassment. I might note that most if not all Big Ten bands had a similar reckoning at some point during this period. For us, it turned into a positive. We reset our course before anything seriously bad happened.

~

The year 2008 also marked my fortieth year as marching band director, and my friends in the University of Wisconsin Alumni Band Association celebrated the occasion by launching a fundraising campaign they titled Project 40. The idea was to replace our grass practice field at the corner of Walnut Street and Marsh Terrace, west of the Natatorium, with artificial turf similar to what is used in Camp Randall Stadium.

I'd mentioned many times how nice I thought it would be if we could replace the grass field, which seemed to always be either muddy or dusty and with the yard lines obliterated. During the fundraising I met often with campus officials to cut through the red tape that accompanies any large project. The land doesn't technically belong to the band: it's under purview of Recreation and Wellbeing at UW. That went well and we received the necessary clearances.

The fundraising kicked off with an initial gift of $25,000 from the alumni band association, whose members knew the difference a synthetic-turf practice field could make.

Dean Teofilo, who played trombone in the band in the early 1980s and was president of the alumni band association in 2008, explained it to *On Wisconsin* magazine:

> There are hundreds of alumni with bad knees because of that field. It was two hours a day, four days a week, and the field was either rock hard or muddy. Plus, our athletic style of marching can really do a number of a field. When we contacted alumni, they realized here was something really worthwhile, and it will ensure Mike's legacy.

The Project Forty redevelopment and upgrade were completed in 2008 at a total cost of $800,000. I was very pleased, although, of course, once you get the synthetic turf, it, too, is susceptible to wear and eventually needs replacing, not unlike uniforms and instruments. Our generous and engaged alumni have long been a great strength of the UW Marching Band.

~

Speaking of anniversaries, our iconic song, "On, Wisconsin!," turned one hundred in 2009. We played a special half-time show in its honor

that October, and in November—the actual month of the centennial—
I gave an interview to the Associated Press in which I reflected on the
song and its legacy.

"One of the things that makes it so extremely popular," I said, "[is
that] the first four bars are so recognizable it almost makes a statement
from the first time you hear it. It says everything in the first four notes."

I noted that we'd played it in a variety of arrangements, including
swing, funk, Latin, and a James Brown–inspired version.

When the reporter asked me to guess how many times we'd play it
across my career, I shook my head.

"It boggles my mind," I said. "On a given Saturday for football,
we'll play it, conservatively, 40 or 50 times including practice. You multiply that by 41 years [of] seven, eight football games in a season. Then
you multiply it for basketball and hockey games, we average eight to
10 times for basketball . . . I don't know if I even want to start to think
about it."

A highly regarded *Milwaukee Journal Sentinel* journalist, Meg Jones,
wrote an article about the one-hundredth anniversary of "On, Wisconsin!" Meg had a good perspective: she'd played drums in the marching
band in the early 1980s.

Since this was 2009, the newspaper also asked Meg to do a video
with some personal recollections of what the song meant to her. She
said that she enjoyed playing it while she was in the marching band, but
that it really didn't resonate any more than "You've Said It All" or "Varsity" or any other traditional Badger pieces. Meg added that it took
on more meaning when she began returning to Camp Randall on one
Saturday each fall for the alumni band performances.

"The coolest time that we play 'On, Wisconsin,'" Meg said of her
alumni band experience, "is during the halftime show. Literally the half-
time show is, they have the regular band, they play and then get off the
field for a short time. Then us old duffs go out, [and] we're kind of
trudging down the field playing instruments manufactured during the
Eisenhower administration. Once we get to our spot and we finish [what-
ever song we're playing], we all turn at one time and face the crowd.

And we go into 'On, Wisconsin.' 'Da, da-da-da-da!' It's so . . . I can't even describe to you what it looks like. Because we turn and you look at the crowd and everyone stands up at one time and it's like this red wave, this tsunami coming at us. People are clapping and cheering and it's electric."

Meg concluded: "I'm not anybody famous. I'm not a star athlete. I'm not anybody that anybody is ever going to cheer for. And yet, for two minutes [during 'On, Wisconsin!'], on a Saturday afternoon in the fall, once a year, I feel like a rock star."

Meg Jones was a sweetheart, someone I really appreciated having in the band. She was one of those kids you never ask twice to do something. More often than not, if we needed something, she'd volunteer.

I'm also far from alone in thinking that Meg was a fine writer and journalist, well known for her work across Wisconsin. We connected again in 2018 when Meg profiled me in the magazine of the Wisconsin Alumni Association. I was terribly saddened in 2020 when Meg was diagnosed with an aggressive cancer and died a short time later. The *Journal Sentinel*'s obituary called her "the heart and soul of the newsroom."

Meg was modest about her journalism success, but I always kept an eye out and was delighted when one of my band members made a mark after leaving UW. In June 2020, the *New Yorker* magazine, in the wake of the police killing of George Floyd in Minneapolis, published an extraordinary fourteen-page spread highlighting the photographs taken by twenty-nine-year-old Isaac Scott during protests in Philadelphia. When a Madison journalist interviewed Scott about the story—the *New Yorker* headline was "A Photographer on the Front Lines of Philadelphia's Protests"—one of the first things Isaac said was that he played trumpet in the UW Marching Band for four years and went to three Rose Bowls.

~

The one-hundredth anniversary year of "On, Wisconsin!"—2009— was also the year that Union South began an extensive renovation that required us to relocate our pre-football game Saturday "Badger Bash" performances to nearby Engineering Mall.

The bashes dated to 1972, just my fourth football season as marching band director. Union South had opened a year earlier, and given its proximity to Camp Randall Stadium, it was no surprise that many Badger fans found it a good spot to eat and drink and chat in the hours before kickoff. Union manager Merrill "Corky" Sischo took note and reached out to me. Might there be an opportunity for the band to do a pregame performance? Corky and I met a couple of times, walked around, and figured out where it might work for the band. There were more trees in the courtyard than exist now but we thought it was possible.

It was quite informal at the outset. We'd set a time of nine thirty or so, depending on the start time of the game (although in the old days they were consistently at one thirty), the band would assemble, and once everyone was there, we'd get started. It was loose. I don't think there was a microphone for a long time, so I couldn't address the crowd. Still, word circulated. By 1974, several thousand fans were showing up, and as the crowds grew, our performance became more formalized. The crowds continued to grow. For the band, as the excitement of those Badger Bashes ramped up, it helped them flip a switch: OK, it's game day, this is important, let's fire up.

When Union South was redone between 2009 and 2011, I was invited to several meetings at Memorial Union where we discussed how the design might best incorporate our Badger Bash performances. Originally I hoped to build tiers so we could get the whole band into the space. They didn't quite have room for that. But they built a platform, and the new southwest plaza at Union South is roughly double the size it had been.

We discussed numerous things people might be surprised to learn were considered. Where would the band gather on arrival? Would the band make an entrance? Again, our options were limited because of the band's size. Paul Broadhead, the facilities director at the Union, really caught the spirit and proposed a bunch of crazy entrances—not for the

band, but for me. At the new Union South I entered in various appara-
tuses, including the Bucky Wagon, with an announcer and microphone
heralding my arrival. It was fun but a lot of work for an entrance that
lasted a few seconds. The band would already be in place. The drums
went in first, then the rest of the band except the tubas, who came last.

In September 2012, we held a fortieth-anniversary celebration of the
Badger Bash. Governor Scott Walker decreed September 15—when
UW played Utah State at Camp Randall—official Badger Bash Day in
Wisconsin. Corky Sischo was on hand to help me cut the fortieth-
anniversary cake.

Ten years on—in early November 2022—I was pleased to be invited
back to Union South to help celebrate the fiftieth anniversary of the
Badger Bash. Corky Sischo passed away in 2017 but it was nice that his
son, Jeff Sischo, was there for the fiftieth-anniversary bash. One of Jeff's
sons was in the marching band under my direction. People were sometimes surprised at how many family members from different generations played in my band. I think the record may be held by the Rooney
family. Bob Rooney was in my very first band (and later active in the
alumni band). Two of Bob's kids and one of his grandkids were in my
band. Three generations! The wife of one of Bob's sons was also in my
band. One show I always wanted to do—I came close one year—was
invite back all the people who met in the band and eventually were
married. It would have been fun. I know of at least one couple who met
in the band, married, divorced, but stayed friendly in part because they
both wanted to come to band reunions.

As part of the Badger Bash fortieth-anniversary celebration in 2012,
the band alumni opened—in the southwest plaza of Union South—the
UW Marching Band Hall of Fame.

Once again, the Union's Paul Broadhead helped make it happen.
I had been meeting with Paul and talking about his idea for a Fifth
Quarter Room inside Union South. At the same time, some band
alumni were talking with me about their desire to honor Ray Dvorak in
a public way beyond the gallery we'd established in the lobby of Mills
Hall in the Humanities Building. My recollection is that I helped put
Broadhead and the band alumni together, and what developed was the

idea of not only honoring Dvorak but establishing a marching-band hall of fame that would celebrate individuals who had made a significant contribution to the marching band throughout its history. It was Paul who suggested the site: outdoors, near the band's location for Badger Bash. Engraved plaques provide brief bios of the honorees and note their band accomplishments. Dvorak and Edson W. Morphy, who was director of UW bands from 1920 to 1934, were the first two honorees, in 2012.

I've referenced the band alumni numerous times during this narrative, and it would be hard to overstate all the contributions they made—financial and otherwise—to our band during my tenure as marching band director. The official name for the organization is the University of Wisconsin Band Alumni Association (UWBAA). From the outset in 2012 the group took the hall of fame inductions seriously, with much thought and consideration given to potential inductees.

The inductees in 2013 were Richard Wolf, who served as codirector of the marching band from 1957 to 1960, and Jim Christensen, a Madison native who, as I've noted, eventually went to work for Disney, after serving as marching band director from 1961 to 1968. It was fitting that one of the most dedicated band alumni members, Robert Tottingham—he served as executive director of the UWBAA from 1961 to 1986—was inducted in 2015. The plaques and honorees now number more than a dozen, and I encourage everyone to check them out at Union South. Two notable inductees in 2016 were my first two female marching band members: Paula Schultz and MaryAnne Thurber.

The most recent class of inductees included William Purdy and Carl Beck, coauthors of "On, Wisconsin!"; Bill Garvey, a music educator I told about in chapter 6; and Gary Smith, our longtime band photographer.

If you've seen photos of the band, or me in my band uniform, odds are Gary took them. Years ago I noticed him showing up at practice, and eventually he asked if he could take some photos. He had a new camera and showed me some of his early shots. They were good. We didn't have any kind of publicity photos and Gary offered to do some. He became our unofficial staff photographer. He did it on a volunteer basis, which was remarkable and much appreciated. We got him into games, bought his film, and took him on road trips. That was his compensation. Over time I'm certain he took thousands of photos. The band kids loved him. There was a period of time, before the internet, when Gary would bring sample photos to rehearsals and the kids would buy them, but it wasn't a money-making deal for him. They only covered the cost of the film. It's great that the hall of fame recognized Gary.

One of the rules for induction in the hall of fame is that individuals be five years removed from active participation with the band in order to be considered. When I retired in 2019, the UWBAA decided to waive its five-year requirement and inducted me into the hall of fame. As you can imagine, I didn't object too strenuously.

~

In 2012, along with seeing the UW Marching Band Hall of Fame debut at Union South, I had a unique opportunity that turned into one of the most exhilarating experiences of my life.

Over the years I had done a few favors for the Naval ROTC at UW–Madison, allowing them to use our band practice field when they didn't have any place else to do their drills. They were grateful, and in 2012 I was invited to be a "distinguished visitor" aboard an aircraft carrier, the USS *George H. W. Bush*, stationed at Norfolk, Virginia.

I spent two days and one night aboard the aircraft carrier, and found much of it of great interest, but unquestionably the highlight was landing in a jet on the carrier's flight deck somewhere out in the Atlantic Ocean. They'd warned me that the jet would stop abruptly and likely give a jolt to my system. *Abruptly* doesn't do it justice. The jet is still going around 150 miles per hour as it touches down, at which point the pilot catches the jet's tailhook on a steel cable stretched across the carrier's deck. The jet is yanked to a stop within about three hundred feet. One hundred fifty miles an hour to zero in a few seconds.

Yes, it was exhilarating. I haven't experienced anything quite like it before or since.

eleven

MATTERS OF THE HEART

The grand reopening of Union South was in April 2011, the same month as our annual varsity band concerts. Our shows that year featured tributes to Motown and the television musical comedy *Glee*. Two of our favorite guest artists returned as well: *Tonight Show* drummer Ed Shaughnessy and the great trumpet player Grant Manhart.

The 2011 concerts also marked the twentieth year that a talented Beaver Dam seamstress named Lois Levenhagen made the sequined suit I wore at the spring shows.

I met Lois in the early 1990s through her daughter, Kathy, who played in the marching band. We'd always hired local seamstresses to measure and alter the band uniforms. I was very fussy about what the uniforms should look like. The pants had to be six inches above the ground. The band hated that—they thought it made them look like they were expecting high water. But once you put spats on, it made the spats more visible.

I don't recall whether we had an issue with a seamstress or had trouble finding a good one, but we had a problem and Kathy said, "My mother does all the seamstress work for the community theater in Beaver Dam. She'd be happy to do our measuring and restitching."

Lois came down from Beaver Dam during registration week for the fall semester. She would measure the kids and take a big pile of uniforms back home to hem the jacket sleeves and pant legs. The kids got to know and like her and appreciate her common sense. She would tell the young women in the band who wanted close-fitting outfits to get a size or two bigger. Why? The uniforms are heavy and warm and feel cooler with a little breathing room.

Early on, Lois came to me and said, "I'd love to design one of your costumes for the spring concert." I knew she was a good seamstress, so I suggested we sit down and brainstorm a bit. I had tended toward the gaudy in my spring concert attire ever since the first one in 1975, when I sweated through my outfit and came on for the second half wearing a loud red-white-and-blue shirt.

One thing I told Lois was "I want glitz."

I'd been going at it haphazardly up to that point. Someone might make me a sequined vest or attach sequins to ready-made clothes. I even went to Las Vegas a couple of times looking to buy something.

Lois said, "Glitz? Let me build an outfit for you."

It was not easy work and she did a great job. You can't sew through a sequin. If you sew too fast you can break a needle. My suits could take from fifty to a hundred hours to produce. There were other things Lois had to learn to factor in. I would have a cumbersome safety harness on underneath that was necessary for my flying routines, so Lois couldn't just do the outfit by my measurements. Neither could I just have a regular pair of pants. When I was airborne the pants and coat would separate, so Lois had to design pants that came up almost to my chest. We learned a lot. She had to cut a slit on the hip so the flying apparatus could fit through and allow me to rotate on it. I like waist-length Eisenhower jackets but I couldn't wear those: it would expose the flying apparatus. Every jacket had to be blazer length.

Just like the entrances, my outfits became a source of anticipation and amusement at the spring concerts. There was pressure to keep topping ourselves. Lois and I would weave our ideas together and take the theme of that year's concert into consideration. We'd keep the costume design a secret, and Lois would make a point of hiding it in a garment bag and personally delivering it to me on the day of the first show.

Lois retired from working with the band after my last spring concert. It had been twenty-seven years. I asked her to come out onstage that last year and deliver my jacket in front of the audience. She was nervous about doing that but I think she appreciated the well-deserved applause she received.

When it came to clothing, I had several superstitions. Elroy Hirsch had given me a pair of red suspenders my second year in Madison, and I always wore them with the marching band. I also always wore the same necktie—with a Windsor knot—until Phyllis told me it had to go. I was upset and threw it away but continued with another one.

On football Saturdays, I always had to have a brand-new pair of white gloves. I didn't mind when they got dirty, but they had to be new when I put them on for the game.

I also used the same whistle for probably the first three decades of my time in Madison. I brought it with me from Butler, where I'd discovered the drum majors used a whistle called the ACME Thunderer.

It was a metal whistle, of course, and I liked the pitch of it. It was produced in the United Kingdom and was first developed in 1884. At one point it was also known as the "Titanic whistle" because the doomed ship of that name used it.

Mine wore out about halfway through my time in Madison. They don't last forever. I think the little cork ball inside goes a bit soft and the sound doesn't have the same trill.

I sent away to the United Kingdom for a new one, but—and this will tell you something about me and superstitions—I continued to carry the first whistle in a pocket of my game day uniform until I retired.

My routine on those Saturdays was always the same. I changed from practice clothes to my band uniform at the Humanities Building, then walked exactly the same route to Union South for the pregame show. I always wore the wristwatch the athletic department had given me after the first Rose Bowl in 1994. After the 1999 Rose Bowl, they gave me a ring, and I always wore that too.

After the game and the Fifth Quarter, I made a point of shaking hands with every band member as we made our way to the Humanities

Building for dismissal. I started doing that my first year in Madison, when the band was pretty small. I knew I could be demanding, expecting a lot of them, and I felt the handshake was a way of saying thanks for making the effort and doing your best. Today we'd probably say I was bonding with them. I did that after every game, even bowl games. If we were going back to get on the buses, I still found a way to shake everyone's hand. I did that until my very last game. It was important to me. I don't know if it was important to them—I think maybe it was. But it's something I did absolutely every time.

I always did another thing before the final home football game each season. No matter the date, I would show up at the last band rehearsal eating an ice cream cone. It didn't matter how cold it was. I did it my first year, when the last game was in late November. The kids had been complaining about the cold all week, so I went to Babcock Hall and bought a big double-dip ice cream cone and brought it to rehearsal. While they were shivering I took a bite and said, "It's all in the mind."

It was a statement about toughness, humorous in a way but with serious underpinnings. It became expected of me at that last rehearsal of the season. One year—it might have been Thanksgiving weekend—Babcock was closed and I had to find a convenience store that was open and buy a Drumstick so I could continue my ice cream tradition.

~

The band required mental toughness but physical toughness too. All that marching took a toll. At one point—sometime around 2010—I mentioned to Dennis Helwig that we were having numerous kids sidelined by things like ankle sprains, blisters, and dehydration. Dennis was director of athletic training services for UW.

He said, "We have all sorts of apprentice trainers. We'll be happy to provide one for you."

I jumped at the offer. We arranged to have a trainer come to our practices two days a week, on Wednesdays and Fridays. They set up a table and were available to make assessments if someone was having a problem. They would tape ankles or do whatever was required. I worked the kids hard because I wanted to weed out those who weren't all-in. I also wanted to take care of those who were truly committed, and the addition of the trainer helped to that end. The kids appreciated it.

~

One regrettable incident occurred during a 2013 Packers game when the band had been invited to perform at Lambeau Field. The visiting team was the Detroit Lions, and at the end of our pregame performance, one of their players started heckling the band. I was near midfield and didn't hear it personally. The band was in the end zone, preparing to play the national anthem.

Lions center Dominic Raiola started yelling profane and homophobic insults at certain members of the band. When they talked about it to me later, they were quite shaken. It was a classless thing to do. Ironically, Raiola's brother, Donovan, had been a standout center for the football Badgers in the early 2000s.

One band member who had been targeted by Raiola described what happened in a Facebook post that was soon picked up by the traditional media:

> [Dominic Raiola] went off on a verbal tirade, among other things, questioning my sexuality (as a band member) and then continued on to bring my sister and my recently deceased mother into the conversation.
>
> After I refused to give him the satisfaction of turning to look at him, he switched targets to a trombone, ranting at him calling him overweight and saying he can't play a real sport. After our halftime show, the same fine gentleman called a female member of the band [a profanity].

On the Monday after the game, Lions president Tom Lewand called me with an apology on behalf of the team. (It wasn't Raiola's first inappropriate outburst: he'd twice earlier been fined for gestures or vulgar language directed at fans.)

Raiola himself called me on Tuesday. He apologized and said he'd been trying to get himself fired up for the game. Our chat was brief. He asked if I'd accept his apology. I said, "Yeah." My thinking was we might as well move on.

I should stress that our overall experience at Lambeau—from playing there the first time in 1989 to our last appearance under my direction in September 2018—was highly positive. We played at Lambeau nearly every year, missing only a couple when the schedules didn't quite work out. The kids always looked forward to it. A Lambeau visit might not have had quite the intensity of a Rose Bowl, but it was special—and the incident with Raiola didn't change that.

⁓

It's also true that for every mean-spirited episode that occurred in the band's orbit, we had one hundred positive ones. In July 2015 I received a call from a *Washington Post* reporter who had seen a viral video that so impressed her she thought the *Post* readers would appreciate hearing the backstory.

A woman named Ann Trachtenberg had been undergoing chemotherapy at the University of Wisconsin Carbone Cancer Center. She'd jokingly told her family that she felt it would be appropriate, as she was leaving the hospital after her final treatment, if a marching band was on hand to play. One of her nieces seized the moment and contacted our band. I didn't recall it specifically, but we tried to do short, feel-good, charitable gigs when we could. Sometimes I'd get the call, sometimes just some band members would hear about it and take the initiative.

The *Post* reporter told me the video of half a dozen or so band members playing as Trachtenberg left the hospital—afterward, she hugged one of our kids—had been viewed ten thousand times since the Carbone Center had posted it. What's not to like about that?

More positives: During the first half of the 2010s, the band marched in three consecutive Rose Bowl Parades! The football Badgers made it to Pasadena in 2011, 2012, and 2013. People would ask if it got to be old hat for the band, and I think the answer is no. Maybe it wasn't quite as big a deal for fans who may have gone to the Rose Bowl in 1994, 1999, and 2000, but no matter what, as soon as the band lands in California, the Rose Bowl committee reminds you that it's serious business. The intensity level rackets up immediately. I did have one assistant who by 2013 said, jokingly, "Oh, Disneyland *again*?" Some of the excitement may have diminished just a bit by then. Me? I would have liked to go to *five* Rose Bowls in a row!

After my retirement, I had a unique opportunity to have a hand in the 2023 Rose Bowl, when I did the arrangement for a song called "Beautiful Wisconsin"—a melding of "America the Beautiful" and "On, Wisconsin!"—that was performed in the Rose Parade by the Wisconsin Northwoods Marching Band, a collaboration band made up of more than four hundred students from more than half a dozen northern Wisconsin high schools.

Amy Kauzlaric Wainscott, who grew up in Eagle River, Wisconsin, was the 2023 president and board chair of the Pasadena Tournament of Roses Foundation—hence the invitation to the northern Wisconsin bands. I'm sure it was the experience of a lifetime for those band kids.

It always was for us, and as a band, we wanted to be careful never to take anything for granted—and that especially included travel. Some fans wrongly assumed the athletic department funded all our trips; on many occasions, we had to find the resources. That's one of the reasons it was a big deal when the spring varsity band concerts started to generate significant revenue. The same with our spring run-out concerts at high schools. Nevertheless, fans were puzzled when the band didn't go to Houston for the opening game of the 2014 football season when the Badgers played highly rated LSU. Or when we had to make the difficult decision to leave the freshmen behind when the Badgers played in the 2015 Holiday Bowl in San Diego. The university told me I could take two hundred band members on the trip. It was a disappointment and bad for morale, but I told the freshmen they'd likely get their chance in the coming years—and they did.

∼

It was at a subsequent bowl game—the 2017 Cotton Bowl in Texas, when the Badgers faced Western Michigan—that I noticed I didn't have my normal amount of energy, and sometimes found myself short of breath.

I'd had previous health issues, as had other members of my family. It's part of life. I choose to mention it here partly because sometimes people who are ill can feel alone, as if nobody else is coping with what they are, unfortunately, having to deal with. But we all deal with adversity. That recognition alone often helps—as will staying as positive as one can.

In 2004, I was diagnosed with prostate cancer. It was never made public, and it came not long after my wife, Phyllis, received a diagnosis of breast cancer. Phyllis had surgery and one of the first things she did was ask—well, she did more than ask—our three daughters to all get tested. Within a few months, one of my daughters required surgery as well. It's a humbling thing, a wake-up call that in a sense we are all pretty fragile, whether we look it or not. Phyllis didn't lose her hair with her treatments. My daughter Milinda did, and a couple of her siblings, Erik and Milissa, had their heads shaved to show support. I participated in some charity events for breast cancer research and was cheered that Phyllis recovered very well.

But any cancer diagnosis is frightening. My prostate cancer diagnosis came about a year after my daughter's breast cancer. I stayed optimistic and, after reviewing all the choices with my doctors, chose radiation treatments rather than surgery. I received the treatments in June 2004—purposely, as it is a slow time for the band and my other duties at the university.

When I came home from the Cotton Bowl in early January 2017 and mentioned my shortness of breath in Texas to my family, they insisted I get a medical checkup. I figured it would be routine. I was given a stress test—walking on a treadmill where they increase the pace—and I didn't do nearly as well as I had on previous similar tests. It turned out I had two blockages. The doctors strongly advised heart bypass surgery. In fact they wanted me to stay in the hospital and have the surgery as soon as possible. I reluctantly agreed. It was a Friday, and they would perform the surgery the following Monday. That gave me two days to lie in the hospital bed and think about it. I also thought about all the things I had planned to do that weekend—a January weekend when there wasn't a lot happening with the band or school and I'd planned to work on other projects. That didn't happen. That's life.

The surgery was on January 24. It went well. I don't remember any pain. What I really recall is being astonished when they expected me to get up out of bed and walk around the very next day.

I said, "You don't really want me to do that, do you?"

They did.

I had some inpatient rehabilitation at Oakwood Village Rehab Services in Madison. There was no public mention. Because it was January and February, a time when, again, there was not a great deal of activity for the band beyond some basketball and hockey games, I didn't have to cancel many personal engagements. My assistant band director, Darin Olson, covered some things for me, as did Sarah Marty, a terrific arts producer who was a top assistant for me at the varsity band concerts for nearly two decades. Sarah even taught one of my classes while I was laid up.

Darin told the band I would be taking a little time away. We downplayed it. He basically said that I had a medical issue and would miss some rehearsals, but everything was fine.

Perhaps not surprisingly, people eventually began learning more. That included the band kids. What that meant, of course, was that my first rehearsal back was filled with emotion. It was mid-March when I came back. I think the band half-expected me to be wheeled in. But I walked into Room 1341 of the Humanities Building, where we had all our rehearsals at that time, and the kids cheered and some cried and I'm pretty sure those were tears I was blinking away myself.

The spring concerts were only a month away. I'd been rehearsing the band for those shows by proxy, communicating back and forth with Darin and Sarah. We really weren't sure when I was coming back. Truth is, my physician, Dr. Charles Stone, would have been happier if I'd stayed away a bit longer.

He said, "Listen to your body."

I was itching to get back. The one ironclad restriction was that I wouldn't be doing my usual aerial stunts at the varsity band concerts. The Kohl Center was a no-fly zone, at least where I was concerned. We were able to rig a couple of things that enabled me to elevate without doing anything but stand.

We'd decided earlier on a theme for the shows, "Nobody Does It Better," which of course is a song from a 1970s James Bond movie. I told the band it was a tribute to them. They turned it around and began applying it to me.

Lest anyone feared the 2017 shows would be maudlin, we dismissed that notion right from the outset. Whereas in the past I'd always first come onstage in some eye-popping, crazy way, this time I entered somewhat uncertainly, slowly shuffling, head down, using a walker. I'm not sure what the audience thought. Once I made it to the center of the stage, I looked up and grinned.

"Oh, the hell with it," I said, and then tossed the walker to a waiting stagehand. The crowd roared.

∼

Just two weeks after our 2017 varsity band concerts, I served as grand marshal for the thirty-sixth annual Crazylegs Classic, a UW athletics fundraising run (or walk) that begins on the Capitol Square and ends inside Camp Randall Stadium. It's named, of course, for Elroy Hirsch, who attended every race up until his death in 2004. Given my friendship with Elroy, I was honored to be asked. I'd helped out at the race in years prior, at both the start and the finish. Some band kids pushed me to actually run the race and I considered it, but that never happened.

That June, the Wisconsin Chamber Orchestra played its twenty-fifth annual Concert in the Park in Portage, and the conductor, Andrew Sewell, included in the program several arrangements of traditional UW songs I'd done earlier for David Crosby, the orchestra's previous conductor. I think Andy was going through the orchestra library, discovered my arrangements, and decided to include them at the June 2017 Portage performance.

I was honored. Arranging music for a professional orchestra can be daunting. There's ego involved when you reach that level of playing. They're good and they know it. There's an old joke about professional musicians: How many trumpet players—or any instrument—does it take to screw in a light bulb? The answer is two. One to screw it in and the other to say, "Oh, I could have done that better."

I didn't get any of that, likely because Andy Sewell, in keeping with his personality, introduced the pieces to the orchestra the right way. The audience in Portage loved hearing them, as they had at Concerts on the Square in Madison when David Crosby conducted.

In June 2022, I was honored again when the Madison Symphony Orchestra asked me to serve as honorary chair at its annual Concert on the Green, a fundraising golf outing at Bishops Bay Country Club.

After golf, members of the symphony played a concert, and I was invited to the podium to conduct for perhaps ten minutes of the program. That was a joy. There was also a remarkable solo performance by a sixteen-year-old violinist named Clark Snavely, who had won the 2022 Bolz Young Artist Competition.

In June 2017—the month the chamber orchestra performed my arrangements in Portage—a new class of twelve was announced for the University of Wisconsin Athletic Hall of Fame, with the induction ceremony scheduled for the fall. It was a stellar class, and I was humbled to be alongside Rose Bowl–winning quarterbacks Brooks Bollinger and Darrell Bevell. I was inducted in the "special service" category.

~

Due to the awards and honors and special invitations, on one level 2017 was a good year for me. But on a deeper and much more important level, it was a very difficult time.

One of the reasons I went to Oakwood to rehabilitate after my heart surgery was that by early 2017, Phyllis, the love of my life and wife of more than sixty years, would not have physically been able to assist in my rehab. She'd been fighting her own health battle for two years.

It began with her having trouble with her balance, which led to some difficulty walking. Phyllis loved bowling but she was not a super-active person, so this early difficulty did not cause us undue alarm. We chalked it up to getting older and tried not to worry. But then one of the doctors made a diagnosis of early-stage Parkinson's disease. She began to deteriorate. It was difficult, but we were heartened by people who stepped up to help. It was indicative of the difference Phyllis had quietly made in many people's lives during her time in Madison.

She never sought the limelight and was quite content to have it shine on me. In one of the few newspaper interviews Phyllis gave, to the *Wisconsin State Journal* way back in 1983, she gave a slightly humorous description of our family life:

> We met in seventh grade. Both of us played trumpet in the junior high band. . . . I was 18 when we were married and worked to help put him through school. We had busy times, but we're really an easygoing family and Mike is very relaxed at home. No, he doesn't help much around the house, outside or inside. And, yes, Mika [our oldest daughter] and I go to all the football games. . . . Our younger children [enjoy] the hockey games. It's always a busy season in the fall, and like the football coaches' wives, I see little of Mike then. He does his thing, I do mine and we get along great.

Phyllis spent nearly three decades working with the Middleton–Cross Plains School District. At the time of that 1983 interview, she was a teacher's aide in early childhood development and special education at Sauk Trail School in Middleton.

She was certified to teach and worked many years with special-needs children. Once our own kids were in school all day long, maintaining a teacher's schedule was a perfect fit for Phyllis. When our kids were headed home, so was she. And she loved special education work. I could never have done what she did. Her patience and know-how were remarkable. I continue to admire people who do that work very much.

Once our kids were married and having their own kids, Phyllis greatly enjoyed her role as grandmother to grandchildren Kami Jo M. Sanner, Michael Barton Mitmoen, Turner Michael Raymond Wilson, Holden Michael Kahlenberg, Raychel Caroline Wilson, and Alex Robert Kahlenberg; step-grandchildren Joshua Ryan Wilson and Courtney Rae Gehlsen; and great-grandchildren Lyra Jo Sanner, L. Apollo Sanner, and Luna Adeline Sanner.

Over the years Phyllis had a good relationship with my band kids. She never wanted to seem to be meddling, but she was always ready and willing to help. She had almost a sixth sense about how and when she might be helpful without constantly hovering around. Phyllis recognized that my mother tended to hover, and to Phyllis that wasn't a positive thing. She very much did not want to be seen as being in the way. But if there was a need, she would step in.

Phyllis enjoyed the tradition the band had of dressing in costumes for rehearsal around Halloween. She would dress up herself and come down and hand out little candy bars—it was an annual tradition. At one point the kids in the band had a big quilt made that said Band Mom. That meant a lot to her.

As Phyllis's condition worsened, we still tried to make the best life we could for her. We moved into a single-level house that was specially built for people with ambulatory problems. It had a huge bathroom with a walk-in shower and doors that accommodated a wheelchair. I didn't want her to feel stuck at home. We hired a ride service that had a van with an elevator so we could still go to concerts and our daughters could take her to basketball games at the Kohl Center.

We even got Phyllis to football games at Camp Randall. The university people really took care of her. The athletic department has always done a good job of providing for people who have limited ability to move around.

We were able to continue what had always been a tradition for us: Phyllis would be by the tunnel in the moments before the pregame started and watch as I brought the band onto the field. She did that, even in her wheelchair. My son-in-law John Mitmoen is a big guy, and he could push her up and down ramps and then get her settled for the start of the game. Eventually she was given a seat in the press box. She would stay all the way through the Fifth Quarter.

Phyllis's birthday was July 12, and shortly after her eighty-first birthday in 2017 she took a turn for the worse. What had been a gradual decline steepened abruptly. On the morning of August 8, I was in my office when my daughter phoned to say they were taking Phyllis to the emergency room at University Hospital. I went over immediately. I guess Phyllis had decided it was time and she went quickly, surrounded by the people she loved most, and loved her most.

Our obituary for her noted her role as a loving and beloved wife, mother, and grandmother, and also included this:

> Phyllis loved to travel, and even short rides were made into an adventure. Whether it was a family trip to explore, a trip to find a donut, or special chocolate treat, Phyllis loved to be in the car. She loved annual trips to New York and Vegas to play the slots and was always up for a ride to find a garage sale. Phyllis loved sports, especially University of Wisconsin Football, and everything red and white.

My wife believed in signs all her life, and on the day of her funeral, our daughters observed a unique cloud formation circling above. A sign? They took a photograph of the clouds that we look at to this day.

twelve

STEPPING AWAY

I was heartbroken, but it was August, which at least meant I was busy and my mind was occupied with the work I had to do getting another marching band season organized.

The football Badgers had a very good year and were invited to play in the Orange Bowl on December 30, 2017, against the University of Miami Hurricanes. It was very much a home game for Miami. And as much as our team and fans were glad to go to South Florida in late December, the bad thing about the Orange Bowl from the band's perspective is that bands don't perform at halftime.

The Orange Bowl is famous for its half-time extravaganzas, and I believe bands have played at halftime only a few times, due to weather. In 1992, for instance, a torrential rainstorm meant they canceled the planned laser light show and the bands played.

We didn't play at halftime but we did get to play a full show before the game. And the day before, the bands from both schools were invited to play at a pep rally at a big park in South Beach, between Ocean Drive and the Atlantic Ocean. I suppose the beach was no big deal for Miami's band, and they declined to participate. We were supposed to play fifteen or twenty minutes, and the organizers asked if we could extend it. We ended up playing for an hour and the crowd—nearly all in red—loved it. The next night, the Badgers iced the cake, with a 34–24 win over the Hurricanes.

By the first half of 2018, I was fairly certain that the 2018–19 school year would be my last as marching band director at UW. I'd had my eye on that timetable for retirement for a couple of years. It would bring my career in Madison to a close at the fifty-year mark, a significant number, a span I couldn't have dreamed of when I arrived in 1969. Fifty years? I was shocked when I first heard Ray Dvorak had held the position for more than thirty. I also wanted to step away while feeling I was still at the top of my game or near it. Having others suggest it was time for me to leave was not anything I wanted to hear.

But I kept my retirement plans to myself for a time. In the 2018 spring semester I kept a vigorous schedule that included conducting the concert band at February, March, and April concerts in Mills Hall. Over the years I'd had administrators suggest I give up those concerts. I wanted to keep them, for a few reasons. The musicians in the concert band were very good musicians, and many likely felt they should have been selected for the top-tier wind ensemble. I had to work hard to convince them they were still important, that the concerts mattered. I enjoyed that and the fact I could demand the best out of them, which, as I say, was high level music. At the same time it gave me the chance to remind everyone—especially the faculty—that I could read music, conduct at a high level, and do something beyond a beer commercial.

We also kept up the varsity band run-out concerts at schools around the state that winter and spring. We'd do anywhere between half a dozen and a dozen each season. It gave the band an activity they had to be responsible for, as well as instilling the need for a top performance no matter the size of the audience at the school. "The people who are there," I said, "really want to see you." It gave us a chance to get ready for the big Kohl Center shows as well. We'd do snippets of things we were planning to do at the spring varsity band concerts in Madison.

Those 2018 varsity band shows celebrated the one-hundredth anniversary of Camp Randall Stadium, and it marked a return of my "flying" at the Kohl Center. It was amusing that the stagehands and my technical support for the shows were very concerned and felt I shouldn't fly. I had to go to my cardiologist and physical therapist and get notes from them saying it was OK for me to be airborne. I felt like a little kid bringing a note from home to the principal's office—but it was nice that they were concerned for me.

~

In May 2018, I told the director of the UW School of Music of my plans to retire at the end of the 2019 spring semester. She was gracious, as was the dean of the College of Letters and Science when learning of my plan. I asked one favor of them: I didn't want any public word until I had the chance to tell my marching band—the band that would be my last—the news personally during tryouts that summer. They both said that was fine.

On the afternoon of August 25, 2018, I gathered all the kids who were trying out for the band into a large semicircle on our practice field on the west side of campus. I stood on a stepladder to address them. I knew what I wanted to say—some key points—but I didn't write anything down. It wasn't memorized. It was from the heart.

"This is always my least favorite day of the year," I said. "It's when I have to make some decisions about who's marching and who isn't. Some of you will be marching the first game, and may not march the second game—may not march the rest of the season. That's the process. You're going to have to earn your spot."

At that point many of the veterans in the band uttered, in unison, a visceral grunt. The uninitiated may have wondered what it was about, but I knew. It was their way of saying they liked what they were hearing but didn't want to have to articulate it.

"There will be people who will be disappointed," I continued. "But if you're disappointed, do something about it. I think people around [here] will tell you there's plenty of opportunity to take the next step."

A moment later I said, "If you don't keep up that intensity, you'll lose that spot. That's the process."

I went on: "I know I haven't been around a lot recently. I want to take a moment to explain a little bit. A few weeks ago I found out I had a problem with some medicine I'd been taking, caused a bad reaction, and the doctor told me I shouldn't do anything for a couple of days."

I paused. "First thing I tried to do was find a new doctor."

The kids laughed.

"Basically they told me to take it easy and not do anything for a while. That's the reason I've not been here. It was hard. But what I would say is I was so delighted with what Darin [Olson] did filling in. . . . He made it work. I was worried. Not about him—but because I thought you might take it as an opportunity to slack off."

I was proud of them and said so. "You didn't. That's what we're about. When it comes time to do the job, we do the job."

Then I got personal. "It's been a difficult time in my history recently," I said. I could feel emotion bubbling up, but I went on. "I don't want to recount a lot of it, most of you know about it. I think the most difficult thing . . . a year ago, when I lost the love of my life. We'd been married for sixty-two years. We started going together in the seventh grade. Can you imagine anyone putting up with me that long?"

I managed a smile and said, "I wish each of you . . . that kind of relationship in your life. I hope that you do."

I then moved into the crux of what I wanted to tell them. It wasn't without emotion, either.

"The thing I wanted you to hear me say," I began, "is last May, I made a decision. This is going to be my last year. I'd hoped my last year would be one where I could go out saying I think I still have a few years left in me. That train may have left the station a long time ago."

That brought some laughter, never a bad thing. But I could tell they were starting to digest what I had just told them. They would be my last marching band.

"But nonetheless," I continued, "no one knows about this decision now, except a few people in the university hierarchy. There will be a press release today or tomorrow, but you're the first ones to know."

I said I'd made that request of the university administrators, and they'd honored it.

"I want you to be the first because you're special," I said. "You're special. I don't care whether it's because you're in the band for the first time or never been in the band until you walked on this field last week. You're special. This band is special."

I wiped a tear as I explained there would be a search committee to find my successor, and that I would not be involved in that search.

"What I hope to hear from you is that this band won't change," I said. "It might change in the way you do little things. Because when I came fifty years ago, you should have heard the uproar when I said, 'We're going to do this.' They said, 'We're going to do *what?*'"

I told them that, of course, some things would change with a new director. But I added that I hoped they'd maintain the important traditions—especially the intensity and desire that made our band special.

"Everything that everybody for the last fifty years has brought to this group," I said. "I will be sorely disappointed if I see that doesn't happen. It's in your hands. It's in your hands to do."

Pointing to only the immediate future, I said, "I'm hopeful we can have business as usual, but I know that's not going to happen."

I again mentioned maintaining intensity and added, "But keep the fun in it. It's supposed to be fun! But you can't have fun without excellence. I learned that a long time ago. You can say you're having fun, but if you don't have that sense of excellence in what you do, it's not fun. It's just going through the motions."

I concluded by reminding them about the importance of recognizing and appreciating the moments of happiness that carry us through the inevitable rough patches that life presents.

"Live for those moments of happiness and remember them," I said.

I then asked—spontaneously, I hadn't planned it—my drum major, CJ Zabat, to get the band ready to play "Varsity." I stepped off the ladder, and joined arms with my band, my last band, as they played the iconic song.

The next day's *Wisconsin State Journal* had a story about my planned retirement. The word was out, which meant that throughout the football season, well-meaning people would remind me that I would be doing some aspect of the marching band experience only "three more times," or "two more times," and so on. I honestly think other people may have been more cognizant of it than I was. I was busy putting together the best shows I could.

Soon after my pending retirement was announced, I was approached by Wisconsin Public Television—they'd earlier asked if they could record some events marking my fiftieth anniversary with the band. Once my plans to step away were made public, they revised their request and asked to be allowed to cover the band and my activities through the 2018–19 season. The resulting documentary covered it all, including my final appearance in April 2019. They were there for rehearsals and performances. They did interviews with band students, alumni, campus leaders, band fans, and my assistants.

The producer was the highly talented Holly De Ruyter. She was as serious about her craft as we were about the band. Holly did a marvelous job putting all the pieces together, and "Mike Leckrone: Wisconsin's Showman" not only pleased me very much but brought Holly a Midwest Emmy Award nomination.

In November 2018, a *State Journal* reporter asked if she could follow me around on the second-to-last home game, for a long front-page story that appeared two weeks later on the day of my final home football game as band director.

I chuckled when I read the story later, which began with us gathering near dawn at our practice field, the temperature at thirty-seven degrees, and me shouting a greeting to the band with my headset microphone: "Good *moooooorning*, Elm Drive!" in the manner of Robin Williams in the film *Good Morning, Vietnam*. I'd started that back when we were still doing our morning, game-day rehearsal at Camp Randall, where my greeting would be "Good *mooooooorning*, Breese Terrace!" I kept doing it once our game-day rehearsals moved to our practice field because the band got a kick out of it and it was my way of saying, "OK, we're back to work now."

My last football game as band director was on November 24, 2018. Two weeks earlier, the Badgers had defeated Purdue, 47–44, in an overtime thriller. Alas, in the season finale against Minnesota, the Gophers came out on top, 37–15.

If the historic nature of the day hit me at all, it was on the way to the dismissal at the Humanities Building, as I shook hands with all the band members one more time.

There was quite a crowd—more than just the band—as I stood on the balcony facing the Humanities courtyard and prepared to make a few remarks.

I began by telling the band we'd have rehearsals the following week, three days for an hour, because there was likely a bowl game in our future, although we didn't know where or exactly when—nor how many in the band would be allowed on the trip.

In part because we knew we were going to have another game, my talk late that Saturday afternoon wasn't as emotional as the one three months earlier when I'd told them about my plans to retire.

I began by recalling that my first football game as band director at Camp Randall, fifty years earlier, the Badgers lost. And the last game, just completed, we lost. Maybe there was some symmetry there.

"I know what happened in between," I said.

"You do too," I continued. "You know what happened between August and now. We got better. . . . And that's what we're about. Getting better is what we're about. . . . I was very proud of you today."

I noted: "I've talked more than I wanted to talk today, had my picture taken more than I wanted to have my picture taken, but I admire you people."

I'd promised them I'd keep it short—after all, they'd be listening to me at the bowl game, the banquet, and the spring concerts—but I did mention a line from *The Music Man*: "What is the good in goodbye?"

To this, I gave a heartfelt answer: There isn't any good in goodbye. "I will miss you greatly," I said. "More than you'll ever know."

∼

The bowl game the Badgers drew, the Pinstripe Bowl in New York City, provided a rematch of the previous year's Orange Bowl in Miami. The Badgers would be playing the Hurricanes, this time in the new (2009) Yankee Stadium, on December 27.

I went to see Todd Nelson, UW's assistant athletic director for event operations, who had an office in the Kohl Center.

I asked Todd, "How many kids am I going to be able to take?"

"All of them," Todd said.

I was very pleased—and also surprised. Taking 280 band kids to New York City was a big financial commitment. My recollection is that Todd said something to the effect that the university wanted me to have a full band for my last football game. I suspect there might have been encouragement from the dean of the College of Letters and Science and even the chancellor's office. Something along the lines of "it's his last game, let's make it memorable."

However it happened, I appreciated it. It turned out to be a great trip, more fun than you might have anticipated from being in New York in December. We went to a Broadway show the night before the game and then on game day, we rehearsed in Yankee Stadium. After rehearsal, the kids got to explore and gained a real sense of the history of the stadium and its predecessor, which had been across the street.

The new stadium has an area behind the fence in center field called Monument Park, which has retired numbers, monuments, and plaques honoring all the Yankee greats through the years. There is also a museum, separate from Monument Park, that features exhibits of Yankee memorabilia, including World Series trophies and rings and a replica of the locker of Thurman Munson, the star Yankee catcher who died in a small-plane crash, at age thirty-two, in 1979.

To top off our New York experience, the Badgers easily dispatched the Hurricanes, winning the Pinstripe Bowl by the score of 35–3.

~

Just a few weeks later, the staff of newly elected Wisconsin governor Tony Evers invited me to Evers's first state of the state speech at the

Wisconsin capitol. They said he wanted to recognize me, and he did, quite nicely, calling me a "Wisconsin institution who embodies both the soul of our campus and the spirit of our state."

Evers and his staff weren't done yet. A few months later, on the Friday of our varsity band concerts in April, the governor made an official declaration that April 12, 2019, would be Michael Leckrone Day in Wisconsin.

It was the kind of thing you wished your parents were around to see. The proclamation was lengthy and filled with "whereases," so I will quote only the last one:

> Whereas, Mike Leckrone's musicality, showmanship, and excellence have brought "Moments of Happiness" to countless students in his music history courses, his concert bands, the UW Marching Band, the UW Varsity Band, and to the extended Badger Band family on the field and in the audience for Very Special Arts Day, UW athletic events, UW band run-out concerts, and public events; Now, therefore, I, Tony Evers, Governor of the State of Wisconsin, do hereby proclaim April 12, 2019, as Michael Leckrone Day throughout the State of Wisconsin and I commend this observance to all of our citizens.

There was considerable excitement preceding the 2019 spring varsity band concerts, again due to the publicity surrounding my retirement. It was certainly exciting for me and the band when all three nights sold out in just a few days.

In preparing the last shows I struggled mostly with keeping the time down to a reasonable length—the temptation is to keep adding numbers—as well as with exactly what I was going to say in closing. I'd always given what I suppose you'd call a recitation at the end of the shows. The band would play background music and I'd say something along the lines of "this has been special. We've had a great year." The wonderful thing was, that was nearly always true. In the last shows I wanted again to pay tribute to the band, be succinct but also not leave anything out. That was a challenge.

My friend Sarah Marty, who helped with the spring shows dating to 2001, will tell you I always want to pack in too much, but my recollection this time is that my production staff kept adding stuff, saying, "You have to do this!" At one point I said, "I want to be home before midnight."

I made my entrance floating in on a replica of the Camp Randall arches. We did numbers from *Jersey Boys*, *Jesus Christ Superstar*, *The Music Man*, and more. There was no way it wasn't going to be emotional at the end. At the last minute we added a solo bagpiper who played "Auld Lang Syne" with a spotlight on him. That was on top of having our traditional last number, another tearjerker, "Elsa's Processional to the Cathedral." I thought about cutting it but was persuaded to keep it.

Wisconsin Public Television livestreamed our last night's show, and I heard later that social media was buzzing with people commenting from all over the country, many of them former band members.

I sang a Willie Nelson song, "Funny How Time Slips Away," toward the end. In my final remarks I said, "I can't thank you enough for all the years." And closed with the lines I always used: "I won't say goodbye, but we'll see you real soon. And On, Wisconsin."

We weren't quite finished. The marching band performed at the Crazylegs run, and the varsity band played at the spring commencement. Both Chancellor Rebecca Blank and the featured speaker—former Badger star J. J. Watt—paid tribute to my fifty years, which I appreciated. The more I thought about it, the more it seemed to have passed in a flash.

That spring I attended, too, my last band commencement party, which is just what it sounds like. The graduating band members tap a keg and invite their families. I attended every band commencement, including the one for my last graduating class. I enjoyed them all. The parents are so proud and can't stop smiling. I think it meant something to the kids that I came, and it meant a lot to me too. The last one helped me draw the curtain to a close.

thirteen

MOMENTS OF HAPPINESS

It was intentional that I not be involved in the effort to find my replacement as marching band director. It was the earliest possible way for me to indicate I would do my best not to interfere with my successor's ability to find his or her own way and make their mark.

I'd seen what can happen when that isn't the case. One of my assistants received a very good band director job at a big university, but the previous band director just couldn't let go and, subsequently, made his life miserable. It ended with my former assistant leaving his new job. That's the last thing I wanted to see happen in Madison.

UW initiated a national search and screened some twenty-eight applicants. In late April 2019 it was announced that Corey Pompey, who most recently had served as the director of athletic bands and associate director of bands for the University of Nevada, Reno, and before that was an assistant band director at Penn State, would be the new director of the UW Marching Band.

In media interviews Corey said he was at first reluctant to apply for the job, citing my fifty years as a tough act to follow.

"I will confess," Corey told Channel 3's Susan Siman, "when Mike announced his retirement, I thought to myself, 'Good luck to that next person.'"

Corey said when he was initially contacted during the search, "my first thought was, 'Thank you for calling. I'm honored, but I'm not going to Wisconsin.'"

Obviously, he changed his mind. "The determining factor in my decision is the legacy that is the Wisconsin band," Corey said.

He continued: "My goal is for the Wisconsin marching band to stay the Wisconsin marching band. My hope is that when people see the band, they recognize it as the band they've known and loved all these years. I'm not looking to reinvent the wheel, and I'm not necessarily looking to take anything away. If we can add something, or if we can enhance something and expand what we're able to do, we'd love to do that."

Now that he's been here a few years, I'm still asked if I get along with Corey. The answer is yes. The way I see our relationship is that I'm here if he needs me to do something, but otherwise it's hands off. I think he appreciates that. I wanted to assure him that I wouldn't interfere.

I'm delighted that Corey thinks some of the features I started are good enough to keep going, everything from when they play certain tunes to the pregame shows. I'm also particularly pleased that Corey and the band seem determined to keep the level of performance extremely high, recognizing the hard work and excellence that are required as part of the equation that also includes fun. They have not allowed that mindset to deteriorate.

They haven't kept everything, but then, neither did I when I showed up all those years ago. I sometimes joke that I was a shock to Ray Dvorak with some of the things I did. It wasn't completely unexpected from his standpoint. We didn't eliminate any longtime, enduring traditions, and Corey, likewise, has maintained those. The kids seem to really like him, and I like what he's doing.

~

I've kept myself busy during retirement, and a lot of the credit for that goes to my association with Sarah Marty and her terrific artistic crew at Four Seasons Theatre in Madison.

In the summer of 2019, Sarah and I and some of her Four Seasons colleagues started meeting for a drink on Monday evenings at the Robin Room on East Johnson Street. One of the draws was Cedric Bae'tche, the Monday night bartender.

A few moments after I was introduced to Cedric, someone said, "You know, he's a really talented musician and artist." He'd done many of the paintings on the walls of the Robin Room. He also turned out to be a terrific guitar player, and is still playing around Madison. Cedric would talk music with our group at the Robin Room on those Mondays, and I eventually began bringing in some of my jazz records I thought he might not know and would appreciate.

At one point I asked Cedric if I might commission a painting from him, and he enthusiastically agreed. I asked him for something that included images of both Louis Armstrong and Bix Beiderbecke on the same canvas. I gave him numerous pictures of them, and what Cedric came up with is really good. I have it hanging in my home.

That fall I started teaching some UW Continuing Studies classes. I did a four-week class on classic big band and dance orchestra recordings that was a somewhat more relaxed version of the undergraduate classes I'd been teaching. I did it because I enjoyed it, and then when the pandemic descended, we switched the classes to online via Zoom. It was all right but I can't say I am a big fan of Zoom. To me it feels artificial.

Once I stopped the online classes I would still hear from people who missed listening to me speak about the big bands and popular music. With Sarah's encouragement I wound up hosting some gatherings in the finished basement of my home, during which I'd play some songs and talk about their back stories and why they were important or meant something to me. Those who attended were former band members and staff as well as other friends who appreciated the music of that era.

One of the musicians who came was Sam Taylor, a colleague of Sarah's at Four Seasons Theatre and a gifted jazz musician. I think it was Sam who one day said, "You know, we could do a podcast."

"What's a podcast?" I said.

I might have been able to fly at the Kohl Center, but technology is not my strong suit.

Sam explained it and said the good thing about a podcast is there were no "hard" time marks you had to hit, it could go as long or short as you wanted.

We agreed to try a dry run—Sam, Sarah, and me sitting around a table in my basement. The subject of the podcast was Louis Armstrong, who, of course, I'd seen play when I was a teenager in Indiana.

The dry run went well enough that Sarah and Sam suggested using it to launch the podcast, which we called *Listening with Leckrone*. We titled the first episode "Hello, Louis! How Louis Armstrong Found His Song."

Sam served as producer and did an excellent job, mixing the music with my commentary and even locating some old Armstrong audio interviews that helped add context. I spoke about Armstrong's early career and the evolution of his style: how Armstrong became Armstrong, long before "Hello, Dolly" broke the Beatles string of number-one hits in 1964.

A little bit more than halfway through the thirty-two-minute podcast, I noted: "Of all the lists of great records I've ever observed, there's one record that appears on almost every list as the most significant jazz record of its period. It's blues, but at the same time, it's uniquely Louis Armstrong. There's one point where he holds a single note, and the interesting thing is holding a note he still manages to swing, which I think says something about the nature of the man itself. This is the 'West End Blues.'"

Near the end of the Armstrong podcast, I told my personal story of seeing him play in Indiana and how impressed I was that he gave 100 percent to the performance, even in a small-town setting, just one more stop on a lengthy tour. What a great lesson that was for a teenage musician to learn. Give your best every time. You owe it to the audience.

We've kept up the podcasts—recordings and transcripts can be accessed on the Four Seasons Theatre website—with episodes on Hoagy Carmichael's "Stardust," members of Duke Ellington's band, many of whom became celebrated musicians in their own right, and more. I closed out 2023 with a podcast on Les Paul, the legendary musical innovator from Wisconsin, followed by an episode on holiday hits. I have a great deal of material and plan to keep doing the podcast indefinitely.

~

In May 2021, I traveled to Oconomowoc to conduct the high school band, which would be playing a piece I composed to honor the memory of Cindy Cernohous, who was Cindy Schwibinger when she played in my UW Marching Band. She also worked as a field assistant for a couple of years.

I liked Cindy a great deal, and at some point after she died, far too young, in December 2018, family and friends in Oconomowoc—her native city—asked me if I would write a piece that could be played for Cindy in memoriam. I agreed and wrote a three-movement piece I called "Joys, Laments, Celebration." I was trying to encapsulate my experience with Cindy: the joy of knowing her, the sadness of losing her, and the celebration of her spirit and memory.

They asked me to conduct it at a concert at the high school. The date was May 20, 2021. I'd been there twice before for rehearsals, which went well. The day of the concert, I stood and conducted the piece, and then, as the last note was sounded, I collapsed on the podium. I lost consciousness but was told later—my daughter Mika and friend Sarah Marty were in the audience—that at first there was a stunned silence. But then a nurse named Teri Krueger, who was a friend of Cindy's and in the audience, came out of the crowd and performed CPR on me. Mika thinks it's no exaggeration to say she saved my life. In any case, I regained consciousness, and promptly angered my daughter by insisting I stay for the rest of the concert. I didn't want those Oconomowoc band kids worrying about what was happening at the hospital while they were trying to play. Once they were finished, I did go to the hospital and stayed a couple of days for observation.

I should note that Teri Krueger, too, had been in my UW Marching Band and is active in band alumni functions. When we see each other these days, we hug.

~

At one point before the pandemic—probably over Monday night drinks at the Robin Room—Sarah Marty and I had been discussing my getting involved in something else with Four Seasons Theatre. This was before the idea for the podcasts. For many years Four Seasons had been doing various kinds of outreach programs at libraries and assisted-living and retirement communities across Dane County. Concurrently they were doing a Great American Songbook series at the Overture Center in Madison. They'd pick a composer—Gershwin, Irving Berlin, Cole Porter—and bring together some singers and a jazz trio for a performance celebrating that composer.

We thought it might make sense to merge the two: bring the Great American Songbook to the facilities where Four Seasons had been doing its highly popular outreach. I would talk about the composer and put the music in historical context in between the jazz trio and singers doing their thing.

The pandemic pretty well scuttled that idea. By the second half of 2021, with the worst of it seemingly behind us, we started talking again. I was, frankly, anxious to do something. Sarah might tell you I missed the applause. I did miss performing, no question. There's a scene in the movie *All That Jazz* when the character Joe Gideon, talking about show business and paraphrasing Karl Wallenda, says: "To be on the wire is life. The rest is waiting."

Sarah and I came up with an idea that was different from what we'd been discussing earlier.

Sarah gave me a DVD called *Elaine Stritch at Liberty*, a one-woman show by the legendary actress and singer that won the 2002 Tony Award for Best Theatrical Special Event. In the show, Stritch mixes tales about her life and show business career with songs that complement the stories.

Could I do that? I thought I could. A mix of band stories, personal stories, and songs. I started with a very rough script, which I put together in late 2021 and early 2022. Sarah brought in Sam Taylor and another Four Seasons colleague, Brian Cowing, to help. Brian's an excellent director and happens to be the grandson of Otto Puls, who was a Big Ten football official as well as the official scorekeeper for Badger men's

After retirement, there wasn't as much time in the rocking chair as I expected. (Leckrone family)

basketball. Sarah also enlisted three excellent musicians for our jazz trio: Chris Rottmayer on piano, Ben Ferris on bass, and Michael Koszewski, on drums.

By summer 2022 we were working on the show in earnest. Much of it was whittling down the number of stories and songs I would have liked to include. Sarah had done cabaret shows. I hadn't, and she kept reminding me that being onstage constantly talking or singing is more demanding than you might expect.

I knew I could tell stories: I'd been doing it for decades at banquets, and people laughed in the right places. Singing was something else. I had a voice coach, Abby Nichols, who was great, but I explained I had three things going against me: singing isn't my main thing, I don't like to practice it, and I don't have that great a voice to begin with. She laughed and we got to work.

In the end, I felt it all came together well. I know I enjoyed it tremendously. We called the show "Mike Leckrone: Moments of Happiness." We did five performances in the Playhouse at Overture in October 2022, filling the seats for most of them. There were a lot of familiar faces in those audiences, a lot of warm feelings in the theater.

The final performance was on a Sunday afternoon. The theater was full. As I had on the previous four nights, I sang "Alexander's Ragtime Band" and other standards. I told band stories, including the thrill of the first Rose Bowl. Of course, there was no way not to tell about riding the elephant into Camp Randall Stadium and having it make a mess on the fifty-yard line, the perfect exclamation point to a dismal era of Badger football.

And I told personal stories: about the first applause I heard as a little kid twirling a baton in my parent's living room in Indiana, and how the sound and feeling of that applause stuck with me.

Putting together that show, and writing this book, required that I reflect on what is now a life of more than eight decades. I realize I've been truly blessed. I had parents who would not allow me to participate in any activity without trying to excel. My dad stressed the value of studying, analyzing, and appreciating whatever was at hand. My grandfather—

FOUR SEASONS THEATRE

MIKE LECKRONE

Moments *of* Happiness

OCTOBER 12–16, 2022
The Playhouse at Overture

Wednesday, Thursday, Friday
& Saturday at 7:30 pm
Sunday at 2 pm

TICKETS: (starting at $20) in person at the Overture Center Box Office in
person, by phone at (608) 258–4141, or online at fourseasonstheatre.com

Four Seasons Theatre made it possible for me to put together a one-man show at the Overture
Center in 2022. (Four Seasons Theatre)

now there was a character—gave me a work ethic and a philosophy of life I still use.

I had some marvelous mentors as well. Fred Fennell, Bill Revilli, Bill Moffit, Fred Ebbs, and Bob Reynolds—all giants in the field of band. I watched and learned up close and in person from such amazing personalities as Louis Armstrong, Percy Grainger, and Duke Ellington.

I recognize how much my family has respected and supported every job I've taken. I feel that at times I was quite lacking as a parent, but the loving bond I have with my kids was always present. I was so fortunate to share my life with my beloved Phyllis, who was a large part of many moments of happiness.

At the end of my 2022 Overture show, I sat and sang "On, Wisconsin!," a quieter version of that wonderful song I had led my band in playing thousands of times.

I love playing and singing that song. I love working hard and preparing and putting on a great show.

I won't say goodbye but see you real soon. And On, Wisconsin.

Acknowledgments

Having a chance to reflect on my life as I worked on this book made me realize just how often fortune smiled on me across the decades.

I hope my gratitude for that is evident in the text. I was fortunate, early, to come from a musical family. I learned how to play music, perform, and do the practice and hard work required to get better.

My learning curve continued later with help from mentors and colleagues at Butler University. I may not have fully realized it at the time, but I was lucky, too, in the timing of my arrival at the University of Wisconsin in 1969. The marching band had a storied history, but the previous decade had seen turnover in the band leadership as well as the virtual collapse of the football program. We had an opportunity to revitalize the marching band as well as launch a varsity band. It was an exciting time. From the outset I stressed hard work and fun. There was plenty of both.

That I stayed in a job I loved for half a century is another example of both great good fortune and, now, a challenge, because there are so many people who deserve thanks for assisting me in that fifty-year adventure. While some are mentioned in the preceding narrative, let me repeat my thanks to all of them, including the thousands of students who marched for me in the band. Sincere thanks as well to the tens of thousands of Badger fans who backed the band with so much enthusiasm. I'd also like to shout-out my assistant band directors, whose dedication and hard work behind the scenes allowed me to focus on putting on the best possible show each time. Thanks to Enrique Feldman, Peter Griffin, Ernest Jennings, Galen Karriker, Gary Kautenburg, Michael Lorenz, Robert Meunier, Darin Olson, Justin Stolarik, Bob Stright, and Frank Tracz.

I was also helped over the years by excellent graduate assistants. Thanks to Terry Austin, O'Shae Best, Richard Birkemeir, Dan Brickner, Louis Cavelli, Gary Ciepluch, Micah Detwiler, Bill Femel, Todd Fiegel, Robert Flum, Nathan Gerlach, Kris Gilmore, Cole Hairston, Thomas Huffmaster, Joe Kieraldo, Craig Kirchhoff, Ed Knesting, Pat Lagulli, Justin Lindgren, Tom Macaluso, Allan McMurray, John Merriman, Jalen Morgan, Gary Owens, Dennis Prime, Olivia Salzman, Kevin Schoeller, Alison Schweickert, Gary Shaw, Nicole Vaughn, David Wallace, James Westbrook, and Ross Wolf.

I had wonderful volunteer field assistants, whose primary assignment was to handle anything I didn't want to do. Thanks to Gary Albrecht, Robert Ancheta, Dave Anderson, Jerry Anderson, Jim Beiersdorff, Scott Beyer, John Biester, Bob Brasser, Patrick Coughlin, John Daniels, Mark DeTurk, Dennis Drews, Arick Ecker, Bill Garvey, Carl Gitchel, Robert Grechesky, Keith Green, Tom Halstead, David Haupert, Tim Hawkins, Dave Heilman, Brian Hettiger, Dave Hoffmaster, Nelson Jones, Barry Kilpatrick, Jim Kutz, Ken Leemon, Phil Lenius, Ray Luick, Steve Matson, Mark Messer, Bill Metzdorff, Steve Morrison, Kurt Mullendore, Doug Neese, David Ohlrogge, David Otterson, Jeff Peronto, Ralph Petersen, Jason Riesterer, Dave Rush, Chuck Sable, Mark Saltzman, Cindy Schwibinger, Gordon Statz, Michael Stone, Karl Strieby, Tom Strutt, Tom Sylke, Jim Tanner, Todd Thompson, Bill Utter, Bill Walker, Tracy Walker, Cal Watson, Matt Whiting, Brian Wilk, and Kirk Zentner.

I owe so much to Phyllis, my wife of sixty-two years until her death in 2017, and hope some of that is conveyed in this book. The same holds for our children, and now grandchildren and great-grandchildren.

My daughters provided an assist by reading and commenting on the manuscript. My friend and colleague Sarah Marty was also helpful in recalling details of our musical collaborations. Jay Rath conducted early interviews with me that helped get the project off the ground. Gary Smith's photographs have long chronicled the band's journey and enrich this book as well. Thanks to Pat Richter for his gracious foreword.

Conversations that appear in the book are drawn from my memory, abetted in some instances by newspaper accounts, notes, videos, and the memories of others. The quotes are as I remember them, while realizing an exact word-for-word reproduction may not be possible. My memory was assisted by stories from numerous papers, notably the *Capital Times* and the *Wisconsin State Journal*, and credit is given in the text. I was helped, too, by referring to *Songs to Thee Wisconsin: 100 Years*, a book I edited detailing the marching band's history.

My coauthor, Madison journalist Doug Moe, and I were friendly acquaintances before getting together for this book. We're now good friends. Our nearly weekly meetings across 2022 were a trip down memory lane for both of us, a trip often punctuated by laughter, never a bad thing.

Thanks, finally, to our publisher, the University of Wisconsin Press. There is no better home for a manuscript filled with Badger love and lore, and that ends with the words "On, Wisconsin."